WILL THE EARTH GET BETTER?

OBERT WYETH

WORKBOOK PRESS LLC
187 E Warm Springs Rd,
Suite B285, Las Vegas, NV 89119, USA

Website:https://workbookpress.com/
Hotline:1-888-818-4856
Email:admin@workbookpress.com

Ordering Information:
Quantity sales. Special discounts are available on quantity purchases by corporations, associations, and others.

For details, contact the publisher at the address above.

ISBN 13:   978-1-960752-03-1 (Paperback Version)
                    978-1-960752-04-8 (Digital Version)

REV. DATE:11/18/2022

WILL THE EARTH GET BETTER?

ROBERT WYETH

CONTENTS

ACKNOWLEDGEMENTS

Most of the verses were taken from the NIV Bible:

The Holy Bible, New International Version ®, copyright 1973, 1978, 1984 by International Bible Society.

Copyright 1985 by the Zondervan Corporation.

Anglicisation 1987 by the Hodder and Stoughton Limited.

This edition first presented in Great Britain in 1987.

Other versions:

Holy Bible, New Living Translation ®, copyright © 1996, 2004 by Tyndale Charitable Trust, issued by the Tyndale House Publishers.

The Holy Bible containing the Old and New Testaments the New King James Version. Copyright © 1979, 1980 by Thomas Nelson Inc. Published by Broadman & Holman Publishers, Nashville. Tennessee.

It contains the 1611 version of the Authorised Version for the Holy Scriptures.

When the earth and all its people quake,

it is I (God) who holds its pillars firm.

Psalms ch.75 v3

He (God) breaks the spirit of rulers,

he is feared by the kings of the earth.

Psalm 76 v12

In spite of all this, they kept on sinning,

in spite of all his (God's) wonders,

they did not believe.

So he ended their days in futility

and their years in terror.

Psalm ch.78 v32-33

SUMMARY

The Bible contains all that is necessary for the work and duties of the protesters who object and take exception to what we have today, not even in England but all over the world. They speak out and complain, they appeal to, demonstrate and they disapprove of what is happening. For their reason for carrying out, is they don't want the world to follow on doing what they have made. Their fathers have made a right mess of the world and it can't get better.

When God created the world, he made it as good as it will ever be (see Genesis ch.1). Everyone will be perfect in its beauty, the animals and birds will be faultless as well as the plants and trees. But early on in Genesis, man and woman failed God and sinned. They disregarded the Lord God, took what they should not have done and the Lord punished and cursed them. It was a change for all kinds of animals, bird, trees and man they would all have to die (see Genesis ch.3). Suddenly, the whole world was changed.

When the Israelites came out of Egypt, God met with them on the Mount of Sinai, he presented them with a number of rules, like the Ten Commandments (see Exodus ch.20). Every man was a sinner because he came from Adam and Eve (see Romans ch.7 v14-20). When the Israelites moved into the Promised Land, the prophet Moses gave them strict instructions (see Deuteronomy ch.28). The Israelites didn't do what God had intended for them to do and that led them to be exiled from the land of Palestine.

God knew in the past that every man was sinful so he sent Jesus. He came to rescue his people not only the Jews but all of us (see John ch.3 v16-17). The worst thing that man has done is to destroy the world. They will have to change from being bad to being good (see Romans ch.8 v7-11). It is a decision that every man and women can achieve if they have the faith and live, but the work is different. They all have to go out and speak the truths of God, preaching and teaching the word, not joining in with the protesters because they abuse the authorities and other things.

I have selected a number of passages which are a reflection of what the protesters were interested in. Then you can see how the word of God in the Scriptures reflects what mankind has done, the protesters starting about 4000 years ago! It is not recent, it will happen back in the past, will go on to the present and until the end of the age in the future.

AFRAID

Afraid is to the people as struck with fear and they can't manage.

Some time later, the Lord spoke to Abram in a vision and said to him, "Do not be afraid, Abram, for I will protect you, and your reward will be great." Genesis ch.15 v1 (NLT)

When Judaism started with Abraham; God changed his name to Abram when he was ninety-nine years old (see Genesis ch.17 v1 and v5). He was the first living thing that God had selected and chosen.

God said, "I will establish my covenant as an everlasting covenant between me and you and your descendants after you for the generations to come." Genesis ch.17 v7

Do not be afraid for God will protect you. Abram was an alien (see Genesis ch.12 v1) and didn't understand what the Lord had meant. He went and did the work of the Lord. Sometimes we might be scared and frightened but doing what Jesus had wanted. It is his calling, his mission for us is to follow.

- - - - - - -

Moses told the people, "Don't be afraid. Just stand still and watch the Lord rescue you today. The Egyptians you see today will never be seen again. The Lord himself will fight for you. Just stay calm." Exodus ch.14 v13-14 (NLT)

Moses took all the Israelites as slaves out of Egypt. He was determined that none of them should be left. He took men, women and children; he also took silver and gold, clothing and livestock, both sheep and herds (see Exodus ch.12 v35-39). Into the barren desert, where they avoided the main military and trade routes leading across the Wilderness of Paran and into Palestine because the Egyptians had stations and fortresses along the way. They didn't want to fight because they were slaves and didn't use swords or shields.

Then the Egyptian realised that they had lost all of the slaves and they wanting to take them back again. The Israelites had travelled and camped by the Red Sea. The people were bounded by the sea and the horses and chariots which were pursuing them. The Red Sea which is today is split into the Gulf of Suez and the Gulf of Aqaba. The Gulf of Suez feeds into the Suez Canal which is located into the Mediterranean Sea.

We have today a large amount of people protesting wanting to do something without delay, but the Lord is in control, he would never leave you alone, just be still and watch. Nobody even thought of God's plan but he would rescue his people across the Red Sea and leave the Egyptians floundering in the mud. The chariots couldn't move quickly enough to get out of the way for the sea came over them and they perished (see Exodus ch.14 v21-22, v29-30).

- - - - - - -

Don't be afraid of anyone's anger, for the decision you make is God's decision. Bring me any cases that are too difficult for you, and I will handle them. Deuteronomy ch.1 v17 (NLT)

Why did they get so angry and try to get the people around them to back them up? Each event and circumstance will take a long time to make a difference. Nobody should protest, looking back to our history, it is in the past, what we can do now is to think about it. Why we do such things to add to our understanding? It was the best policy, thinking about the people, the country, the circumstances and the situation of which we can achieve. Whether it is right or wrong.

This is the decision of the Lord, 'bring me cases that are too hard for you and I will decide'. Don't be frightened of anyone's anger. Make sure that what we do is from the Lord and trust him for what is to come.

- - - - - - -

Do not be terrified by them, for the Lord your God, who is among you, is a great and awesome God. The Lord your God will drive out these nations before you, little by little. You will not be allowed to eliminate them all at once, or the wild animals will multiply around you. Deuteronomy ch.7 v21-22

Later, the Israelites will journey to the Mount Sinai where the Lord meets them. They find out about their relationship with God and have added instructions about what they should be doing in the present and future. The Lord will wipe out the nations that were around you.

It was in the Wilderness of Paran. Scrub land with desert all around you it needs faith and courage. It does not stem from the numerical greatness of the people or any virtue of them but on the covenant of God. They have to go forward and drive out the people in the Promised Land. He is a great and awesome God and because the nations were evil and worshipped other gods (see Deuteronomy ch.8 v19-20).

Do not be afraid of them; the Lord your God himself will fight for you. Deuteronomy ch.3 v22

It doesn't mean that the nations will go away. He watches and is aware of what you are doing. It is not fear but the Lord your God will fight against these nations, one by one. He is in control. He knows what the situation is, he is not worried by all the mess you have created in the desert. You will have to wait until he is ready to act. Even your children who do not know what is right or wrong (see Deuteronomy ch.1 v39).

- - - - - - -

God said, "Who is this that darkens my counsel, with words without knowledge?" Job ch.38 v2

Do you know how the earth was created? Who closed the sea up? Have you journeyed even to the stars? What is the abode of light? Why is the lightning so powerful? Do they report to you? Can you bind the stars? Do you hunt with the lions? (see Job ch.38 v4-41)

Job said he couldn't do it. But even now with all our majestic computers and all the necessary hardware, we do not know how the earth came about. But God does, he remembers kindly all the solar system, the plants that made up the trees, the animals, birds and fish and that includes even you.

- - - - - - -

When I am afraid, I will trust in you. In God, whose word I praise, in God I trust; I will not be afraid. Psalm ch.56 v3-4

King David when the Philistines had seized him in Gath. He was terrified, panic-stricken, numb with fright we all would be afraid of what will be coming next. A prayer for help when the Psalmist is attacked by enemies and his life is threatened. It is trust in the face of fear. It is a call to God, help me, please help me! It confesses a deep trust in God and no-one else.

Not even a call to arms, a deposition of the rulers, a mass of agitators with sticks and messages on them. Only the supreme and majestic God will help you.

What can man do to me? Psalm ch.56 v11

Renewed trust in God. You stand out doing nothing but trusting in the Lord. He can do anything or anywhere he wants. He had been there from the beginning when he created the world. The hot earthquakes and volcanoes spitting heated streams out of the earth where man is not even there.

- - - - - - -

King Cyrus decided to win over his peoples of his vast kingdom though tolerance of religious and national feelings. He allowed the renewal of worship which had been suppressed by the Babylonian Empire.

Nehemiah he was a cupbearer to the king, it was about 440 BC. He was allowed to go to rebuild the walls at Jerusalem and he became governor over the peoples there (see Nehemiah ch.1 v11, ch.2 v9, ch.10 v1).

I stood up and said to the nobles, the officials and the rest of the people. "Don't be afraid of them. Remember the Lord who is great and awesome, and fight for your brothers, your sons and your daughters, your wives and your homes." Nehemiah ch.4 v14

Nehemiah said, 'Don't be afraid of them'. He was talking about opposition to the rebuilding the walls around Jerusalem. He quoted the Law of Moses: Remember the Lord, he is great and awesome, fight for your brothers and your relatives and homes. Fear, why do we have a great God who can do everything? The Lord himself will care for our relatives and homes. It seems likely before the people went into the Promised Land.

It is the same God who doesn't change like shifting shadows, who dart around in the dark and move around in the dimly lit streets (see James ch.1 v17).

- - - - - - -

A furious squall came up, and the waves broke over the boat, so that it was nearly swamped. Jesus was in the stern, sleeping on a cushion. The disciples woke him up and said to him, "Teacher, don't you care if we drown?" ... He said to his disciples, *"Why are you so afraid? Do you still have no faith?"* *Mark ch.4 v37, v40*

Jesus was sleeping on a cushion, he was tired, the boat was tossing around in the sea even the waves came over him. But he slept and he was tired. The parables that Jesus taught by the lake: (see Mark ch.4)

> The parable of The Sower.
> A Lamp on a Stand.
> The parable of The Growing Seed.
> The parable of The Mustard Seed.

Jesus got into a boat because of the crowd that followed him. He explained what he came to do and he tried to get the people to follow him. When he woke up, he said to the wind and the waves, 'Be still' and he said to the disciples, 'Have you no faith?' He still had to go on healing and teaching until he finished the word his Father in heaven had given him (see John ch.17 v4).

- - - - - - -

I am leaving you with a gift—peace of mind and heart. And the peace I give is a gift the world cannot give. So don't be troubled or afraid. John ch.14 v27 (NLT)

Jesus said at the end of his life before he was arrested, 'Don't be afraid'. The peace I give is not as the world will give you, don't be troubled or doubt of what is to come. The path of life is not easy for a believer it may involve suffering and persecution or even death (see Hebrews ch.11).

Jesus will give you the peace in your heart and it will take you through. Don't be worried, the end will be worth it. You can have treasure in heaven (see Matthew ch.6 v19-23).

- - - - - - -

But you should keep a clear mind in every situation. Don't be afraid of suffering for the Lord. Work at telling others the Good News, and fully carry out the ministry God has given you. 2 Timothy ch.4 v5 (NLT)

We too are suffering for the Lord Jesus (see Matthew ch.10 v39). We understand that the good news of Jesus whether they think it so or not. We are going out and spreading the gospel: What he was like? How did he live? His teaching and miracles? Why did he die? What happened after that? The resurrection and your soul matters even to Jesus. This is important that you explain the good news to people around you. A clear mind in every situation.

Work at telling the people to come to Jesus. If you don't do it, how can they respond? Jesus tells you to do it (see John ch.17 v16--18).

- - - - - - -

Do not be afraid of what you are about to suffer. I tell you, the devil will put some of you in prison to test you, and you will suffer persecution for ten days. Be faithful, even to the point of death, and I will give you the crown of life. Revelation ch.2 v10

Satan is malicious and cruel and likes to mislead others. Even the news presenters, books and publications, professors who teach and others mock Jesus. You may go to prison to be tempted and persecuted. Be faithful even to the point of death. Speak out and suffer for the Lord Jesus. We all have a job to do for the Lord (see Matthew ch.28 v19-20). Nobody is exempt for the 'Great Commission'.

Don't be frightened or scared. We all will have a job to do.

ANIMALS

Animals including wild beasts, birds and fish, reptiles and creatures that move along the ground.

God made all sorts of wild animals, livestock, and small animals, each able to produce offspring of the same kind. And God saw that it was good. Genesis ch.1 v25 (NLT)

God had planned what he was about to do for the heavens and the earth (see Genesis ch.1 v1). It was demonstrated that the orderliness and reason of God's creative activity. The earth was covered by masses of water and certainly cool. God created the lights in the sky to see the seasons so it is possible that the earth was stationary in the beginning. God created the trees and plants before the animals came on the earth, otherwise they would have no food.

His creative work was finished. It was totally effective, absolutely perfect. It did not have to be repeated, repaired or revised. God said, 'It was very good'. Humans, animals and the trees were perfect and they would live forever, they will carry on fulfilling life located on the earth.

- - - - - - -

But Adam and Eve came along and spoiled it. They sinned against God and did what he instructed them not to do. By going up to the tree of life and eating the fruit to make sure that they thought like God.

Everything was changed:

To everything, "Cursed are you above all livestock and all the wild animals" (Genesis ch.3 v14).

To the woman, "You desire will be for your husband and he will rule over you" (Genesis ch.3 v16).

To the man, "It will produce thorns and thistles for you" (Genesis ch.3 v18).

To the animals, "He made garments of skin for Adam and his wife" (Genesis ch.3 v21).

All the earth was changed in a moment, stars, planets, humans, animals, plants and trees had to die because of mankind's sin.

The sinful mind is hostile to God. Romans ch.8 v7.

Human culture through sinful man has encouraged his proud rebellion against God. Man is against God and nothing man can do to spoil it, he was in enmity against God. He was hostile towards God, he hated everything that God made, he had malice against God's ways. He was evil and cruel. This is what man encouraged. and he has taken it out with all the animals.

- - - - - - -

The Lord saw how great man's wickedness on the earth had become, and that every inclination of the thoughts of his heart was only evil all the time. The Lord was grieved that he had made man on the earth, and his heart was filled with pain. Genesis ch.6 v5-6

Each man or woman today is not to exploit, waste or despoil the animals but to care for them regardless whether they worked on the ground, flew in the air or swam in the sea. God said so, 'Let the people rule over all of them' (see Genesis ch.1 v26). The rules are there in the beginning and are there in the end of time. Man has a duty to all the animals while he is there on the earth. To care for them and look after them.

Each creature whether the animals in the land, birds are in the air or fish in the sea, God would expect man to care for them. The writings in God's book are where we fail to protect and harm them (see Revelation ch.20 v12).

ANIMALS IN THE PAST

With all the animals that were on the boat with you—the birds, the livestock, and all the wild animals—every living creature on earth.   Genesis ch.9 v10 (NLT)

God wiped out all of mankind, plants, trees and animals on the earth but saved Noah his family and animals who were in a boat called the ark (see Genesis ch.6 v17-21).

The animals and birds could repopulate their former habitats.   Sin had brought violence to the earth and because God had now appointed meat as a part of man's food (see Genesis ch.9 v3).   The animals would 'fear and dread' even man's presence as he moved around (see Genesis ch.9 v2).

- - - - - - -

"No," Moses said (to the Egyptians), "you must provide us with animals for sacrifices and burnt offerings to the Lord our God.   All our livestock must go with us, too; not a hoof can be left behind.   We must choose our sacrifices for the Lord our God from among these animals." Exodus ch.10 v25-26 (NLT)

While the Israelites were slaves in Egypt, Moses would argue with the Pharaoh who didn't want the Israelites to leave.   Pharaoh thought they could leave the animals behind.   All our livestock must go with us, we need to sacrifice to our God and Moses was talking about the sheep and herds.   Not a 'hoof can be left behind'.   Pharaoh knew that Moses was not willing to leave his sheep behind and he understood that the Israelites wanted to leave because they were ill-treated by the Egyptians.

- - - - - - -

Do not mate different kinds of animals. Leviticus ch.19 v19

While they were in Mount Sinai, God met them and gave commands and instructions about what they should do in the Promised Land.   He said, 'Do not mate with various kinds of animals'.

A mule is the offspring of a male donkey and a female horse. Mules tend to be healthier, sounder, longer lived than horses. They are extremely affectionate animals. They have a good sense of self-preservation and they combined the strength of a horse with the sure-footedness of the donkey. The mule did not appear until late in king David's reign (see 2 Samuel ch.13 v29) because it was forbidden by the Lord, it was about 250 years later, because God had commanded his people to not mate with different kinds of animals.

Absalom, a son of David was a very difficult child, he was spoilt and rich. He decided to get a mule and he tried to get king David off the throne to make himself king (see 2 Samuel ch.15 and Psalm ch.3). Then after that the mule existed in Israel. Mules cannot give birth of their own, they would be sterile as their chromosomes are not identical with horses. Even David did not read the Mosaic Law, he left it to the priests. Otherwise, he would not have permitted a mule to be in his kingdom.

- - - - - - -

Do not eat any detestable thing. Deuteronomy ch.14 v3

God gave his instructions to Moses about what they could eat and what they should leave (see Deuteronomy ch.14 v4-21; Leviticus ch.11). Especially about animals, fish and birds. Animals that chewed the cud and had a split hoof, fish that had fins and scales, birds and insects are also covered in these instructions to the Israelites. It would be for health reasons to preserve the sanctity of Israel as God's holy people (see Leviticus ch.11 v44). To get the Israelites to regard a clean and unclean foods were intended to separate the people from things that the Lord had forbidden.

There is no Biblical sign of an evolution where one thing turns into another type of creature. Each kind of animal, God created different kinds of animal, each was different from the rest. There is no reference in the Scripture to a dog transferring into a cat, or a lion turning into a bear or a sheep transplanting into a goat. They all had separate 'kinds'.

But ask the animals, and they will of teach you ... Which of these does not know that the hand of the Lord has done this? Job ch.12 v7, v9.

As the work of man develops, like going into war, vaccinations for illnesses, computers to work even faster than mankind can. As men's advancement grows each one has the foreknowledge of the past. We don't have to do it all over again.

Bears, lions and snakes (see Amos ch.5 v19). Frogs, flies, gnats and locusts (see Psalm ch.105 v30-35). Mice and rats (see 1 Samuel ch.6 v4-5) and even lion, wolves and leopards (see Jeremiah ch.5 v6). If you have a problem with this fact, ask the animals! They will tell and instruct you that God has created them.

- - - - - - -

He also taught about animals and birds, reptiles and fish. Men of all nations came to listen to Solomon's wisdom, sent by all the kings of the world, who had heard of his wisdom. 1 Kings ch.4 v33-34

King Solomon was indeed special and unique. He asked for wisdom in a dream from God Almighty, to lead his Israelites in what they should be doing. The Lord approached him and asked him what he should be given. He didn't ask for long life, wealth or the death of his enemies. So God gave him a wise and discerning heart. Nobody could match him today with all the computers and software. He knew on what to do with the animals and birds, reptiles and fish. He explained how they find food, their nests and dens, how animals get together to mate, their lives so short and how to manage them.

ANIMALS IN THE PRESENT

Your righteousness is like the mighty mountains, your justice like the ocean depths. You care for people and animals alike, O Lord. Psalm ch.36 v6 (NLT)

God cares for his people and animals alike (see Nehemiah ch.9 v6). Many people are like animals, they eat what is around, they lose their homes, they are thirsty for water, the crops failed and they go hungry. It wasn't like that in the beginning when God created all of the earth, he made sure that the trees and plants produced fruit and seed (Genesis ch.1 v11), he gave Adam the job of caring for all of the animals and birds (see Genesis ch.2 v15).

However, mankind sinned against God, so it was a result of sin that man and animals suffer, have diseases and die.

For every animal of the forest is mine, and the cattle on a thousand hills. Psalm ch.50 v10

Look around you, every animal is mine says the Lord. I care and protect them deeply. No sparrow will fall to the ground apart from the will of the Father in heaven (see Matthew ch.10 v29). Even the sparrow, a humble bird it is not coloured, nor even brightly textured, it simply comes to feed its chicks. Even the sparrow needs a home and God will see that it gets one (see Psalm ch.84 v3).

Think about it. It will be God who protects and feeds them (see Matthew ch.6 v26), but God feeds them through men, by putting food or water out in the garden.

The godly care for their animals, but the wicked are always cruel. Proverbs ch.12 v10 (NLT)

The righteous care for their animals but the wicked are always cruel and don't take the trouble of aiding and helping the animals. This marks out the righteous from the wicked, the good and the bad. Jesus talked about the tree and its fruit (see Matthew ch.7 v17-20). The bad tree that does not bear good fruit will be cut down and thrown into the fire. The verses repeatedly indicate, that the bad tree will be sacrificed; the fruit will be bad and that is related to how we treat all animals, reptiles, creatures or birds.

It is expected that we are responsible for how we treat the animals (whether wild or tame, even flies or wasps, we need reptiles and snakes). God will record everything we do and he writes it in his books.

For people and animals share the same fate—both breathe and both must die. So people have no real advantage over the animals. How meaningless! Both go to the same place—they came from dust and they return to dust. Ecclesiastes ch.3 v19-20 (NLT)

People do not have any advantage over animals, they all will have to die and they don't take anything with them. No gold, no houses, nothing of value. Our souls when we die will go to God and we will wait for the judgement to come. What does God think of the care of all the animals? (see 2 Peter ch.2 v9-10).

The people will certainly be judged (see Revelation ch.20 v11-15) but the animals do not. Do you not know when God flooded the earth he rescued all of the kind of animals? He loved all the animals and he created them with all their fur and feathers, coloured markings, each one had a different place on earth. He selected where they should have their home. He didn't want to create and make it again. He selected every kind of animal both male and female.

- - - - - - -

I myself will fight against you with a strong hand and a powerful arm, for I am very angry. You have made me furious! I will send a terrible plague upon this city, and both people and animals will die. Jeremiah ch.21 v5-6 (NLT)

Israel had gone into exile under the Assyrian Empire and Judah was left behind. Where the king Zedekiah was indeed reigning. The four last kings were evil and did not respond to God from 609 -587 BC, a total of twenty-two years! God sent King Nebuchadnezzar to drive them out and export them to Babylon, but he left the poorest people to manage the land.

Everything was gone, the temple of God, the treasuries of the king and his officials, they broke down the walls of Jerusalem and they burned all the palaces (see Jeremiah ch.42 v2). The people waited until 70 years had passed until in the first year of Cyrus, King of Persia. God moved the people back to Jerusalem but it was only a remnant of the people of Judah. It was the children of their forefathers who had done badly in Jerusalem (with false idols. Israelite slaves and ignoring God). The Lord will be very angry. He sent his prophets but they were ignored, men and animals will die in the slaughter of what will come. It will be the same as when the God flooded the earth. Even the poor animals will die because of man's sin.

ANIMALS IN THE FUTURE

Search the book of the Lord, and see what he will do. Not one of these birds and animals will be missing, and none will lack a mate, for the Lord has promised this. His Spirit will make it all come true. He has surveyed and divided the land and deeded it over to those creatures. They will possess it forever, from generation to generation. Isaiah ch.34 v16-17 (NLT)

With the general forecast and woeful agreements on earth, men will be fighting men. God will provide for his animals and birds, they will be looking for a mate. The earth will be trashed and bare, the weapons will be piled up on the ground, there will be rubbish everywhere. But over the years it will seem obsolete we will have to remove it. Like horses to plough our fields or tractors to make it better with wide open spaces or even steam trains that take in more coal and water.

Take what the prophet Isaiah says: (ch.11 v6-11 and ch.65 v17-25)

> Not one animal or bird will be missing.
> The Lord has promised this.
> The Holy Spirit will make it all come true.
> God has surveyed the land and he has divided it.
> He has determined to let the creatures be there.

In the future, animals and birds will still be there, but not with illnesses or disease. They will live forever as in the Garden of Eden.

- - - - - - -

On that day I will make a covenant with all the wild animals and the birds of the sky and the animals that scurry along the ground so they will not harm you. Hosea ch.2 v18 (NLT)

In the future, God has decided to not let the creatures harm you, whether a lion or a bear, the eagle or a hawk they would not cause you injury or damage. God has made a covenant with all the creatures to protect you.

Sinful man has a lot to answer for, the earth will be damaged and the creatures will tell God what you did on this earth. Do not think that the creatures that God has made will be silent? He cares for all the creatures on earth, he notices that one is lame, one is beaten and suffers pain through man (see Job ch.42 v1-2; Psalm ch.121).

Hear the word of the Lord, O people of Israel! The Lord has brought charges against you, saying: "There is no faithfulness, no kindness, no knowledge of God in your land. You make vows and break them; you kill and steal and commit adultery. There is violence everywhere—one murder after another. That is why your land is in mourning, and everyone is wasting away. Even the wild animals, the birds of the sky, and the fish of the sea are disappearing. Hosea ch.4 v1-4 (NLT)

When God removed all the people on earth by the flood though morally innocent, the animal world as creatures under man's corrupted rule shared in the Lord's judgement.

At the final end, the heavens and the earth will be devastated by fire. The heavens will disappear with a roar and the earth and everything in it will be laid bare (see 2 Peter ch.3 v7, v10). Then, the people will come before the Lord to account for their time on earth. What have they done with the animals? They will each come before the God who is sitting on the throne. Everyone will be there, young and old.

How the animals moan with hunger! The herds of cattle wander about confused, because they have no pasture. The flocks of sheep and goats bleat in misery. Lord, help us! The fire has consumed the wilderness pastures, and flames have burned up all the trees. Even the wild animals cry out to you because the streams have dried up, and fire has consumed the wilderness pastures. Joel ch.1 v18-20 (NLT)

This is what it will be like and the fire will consume all the creatures. It will be a dreadful, shocking and consuming place. The fire has taken all the streams and rivers and the pastures where the animals get their food and drink. When you read this, you might be shocked at what God had done.

But remember this: God is holy and pure. He doesn't change he is the same, in the past and the future (see James ch.1 v17). When the Israelites complained about their hardships, God's anger was aroused, he sent fire among them and burned them (see Numbers ch.11 v1). He is very angry because he trusted his children to obey him (see Deuteronomy ch.29 v25-28).

It didn't start like that, a vegetation for mankind and the animals but after the flood mankind ate meat. The eagle and leviathan they must eat flesh (see Job ch.39 v30, ch.41 v33). Some animals kill, some graze and other filter food from water. Food is important as it feeds the body. Some behaviours are built-in or instinctive, but others are learned during the creature's life. The creatures ate meat but in the future kingdom they would go back to a vegetation existence.

I will sweep away both men and animals, I will sweep away the birds of the air and the fish of the sea. The wicked will only have heaps of rubble when I cut of man from the face of the earth, declares the Lord. Zephaniah ch.1 v3

God said it to the prophet Zephaniah in 625 BC. Everything has gone: mankind, animals, birds and the fish of the sea when God will sweep away everything on the earth. There would be heaps of rubble on the ground. The fire will burn up the rest during the heat of the furnace. He said it about 2700 years ago! It is not something new, it would be there in the Scriptures.

- - - - - - -

There are also heavenly bodies and there are earthly bodies. 1 Corinthians ch.15 v40

There would be heavenly and earthly bodies when we have died. Different characteristics but the same soul. Each one will have a new body. When Jesus Christ comes again, all the souls will have new bodies, so they can stand before the throne of God to be judged (see Revelation ch.20 v12). Each one will be standing to attention before God. We all will have to change but the animals too. To be free, to not eat meat, to be there with us.

They will neither harm nor destroy on all my holy mountain. Isaiah ch.11 v9 and ch.65 v25

This is true when we eventually go to heaven, after the judgement and see and rejoice with all the animals. Even a little child will play with them and they would be harmless. They rejoiced and played with animals with us on this earth. We could look up and see the mountain of God.

- - - - - - -

But these people scoff at things they do not understand. Like unthinking animals, they do whatever their instincts tell them, and so they bring about their own destruction. Jude ch.1 v10 (NLT)

Woe to the false teachers who practise deceit in the name of the Lord. They practise error and many people will fall for them. They all will be caught and they are concentrating basically on error. They will be doomed as when the Lord has ejected them from his kingdom. They don't think that animals and birds matter.

But the day of the Lord will come like a thief. The heavens will disappear with a roar; the elements will be destroyed by fire, and the earth and everything in it will be laid bare. 2 Peter ch.3 v10

This is the final day for those who existed on the earth. Mankind and all the animals will be destroyed with a fire. Nobody knows when it will come, everybody would be going around with work, school children will be playing, mothers will be going out shopping and the animals will be sleeping. It will be like a thief coming up to a house when nobody knows when it is there. Jesus will return and then there would be a terrible fire, like when Noah and his family and the animals were on the boat. But sadly, mankind thought the ark was silly, how could the ark get off the ground? It was the same thing as the fire. Everything including the animals.

Jesus said, "Therefore keep watch, because you do not know the day or the hour." Matthew ch.25 v13

The Bible is the key to what is going to happen. But, the so-called important people on earth think that it is impossible to take it seriously, but they will be caught out. Some people have decided that both in Daniel and Revelation they can predict the coming of the Lord. But they were wrong. Nobody knows but only the holy Father in heaven (see Matthew ch.24 v36).

On that day all the springs of the great deep burst forth, and the floodgates of the heavens were opened. And rain fell on the earth for forty days and forty nights ... The waters flooded the earth for a hundred and fifty days. Genesis ch.7 v11-12, v24

The people on earth and the rest of the animals did not realise the quantity of water that could move the ark above all of the mountains. They thought that it was impossible to move the ark as it was so big and strong. Why did it have to happen? Because man has sinned and broken away from God, he created the world and everything in it, so man is a product of his work. Each man dies and so does the stars, the animals, the plants and the trees. Does that not tell you something about God?

The Lord is not slow in keeping his promise, as some understand slowness. He is patient with you, not wanting anyone to perish, but everybody to come to repentance. 2 Peter ch.3 v9

God is waiting until the last moment, when a person might come to him and say, 'I am a sinner, please help me'. Like when Jesus was crucified and the other criminal who was crucified with him:

Then he said, "Jesus, remember me when you come into your kingdom." Luke ch.23 v42

He was saved, because he understood that Jesus had done nothing wrong. He asked him for help while hanging next to him. He didn't have anything to give to him, he only asked him to do something for him. It was only a brief time that he was there while Jesus gave up his Spirit to the Father.

BARLEY AND WHEAT

Barley and wheat are cereal to be consumed by mankind.

God said, "Never again will I curse the ground because of man ... As long as the earth endures, seedtime and harvest, cold and heat, summer and winter, day and night will never cease." Genesis ch.8 v21-22

God promised that as long as the earth continues everything will be normal. Seedtime and harvest will be there, the world will go on circulating around the sun. Nothing can stop the earth moving, even Satan. Still God has given his word that harvest will still continue he has given us this guarantee. We will look at the world and if there is enough food for all, provided they share it out.

For the Lord is bringing you into a good land - a land with stream and pools of water; with springs flowing in the valleys and hills; a land with wheat and barley, vines and fig trees, pomegranates, olive oil and honey; a land where bread will not be scarce and you will lack nothing; a land where the rocks are iron and you can dig copper out of the hills. Deuteronomy ch.8 v7-9

Everything is perfect the Israelites were going into the Promised Land. Wheat and barley and the crops that you grow he has presented to you. Be careful that you do not forget the Lord your God and observe his commands and his laws. The flawless and unmarred place. Where litter and plastics didn't even appear when the streams flowing down the hills were pure and clean. This is what he promised to give to the Israelites. The barley and wheat will still grow there provided you obey the Lord your God.

- - - - - - -

Then let thistles grow on that land instead of wheat, and weeds instead of barley. Job ch.31 v40 (NLT)

Still the enemy was trying to stop that. Satan and his fallen angels to take away what God had promised. Interesting that Job commenting on the crops around him. He knew that the devil and his angels through his painful sores, were trying to make him give up and blame God for what had happened. If you blame God for everything, you might have to face or endure thistles and weeds, rather than barley and wheat.

- - - - - - -

So Ruth gathered barley there all day, and when she beat out the grain that evening, it filled an entire basket. She carried it back into town and showed it to her mother-in-law. Ruth also gave her the roasted grain that was left over from her meal. Ruth ch.2 v17-18 (NLT)

The harvest was barley, it was the first crop that the men brought in from the fields. She was poor and a Moabitess, she had come back with Naomi, her mother-in-law after the famine (see Ruth ch.1 v1). She was going out to work with the harvest, behind all the others (see Ruth ch.2 v3). She worked hard and the men noticed her (see Ruth ch.2 v6). She collected all the sheaves for a whole day, bending down, putting it in her basket, looking for the grain that the men had missed. She beat out the grain, roasted and cooked it. Ruth gave Naomi the grain that was left over for her meal. It is a hard life when you are poor.

- - - - - - -

Bringing the man of God twenty loaves of bread barley bread baked from the first ripe corn, along with some ears of new corn. "Give it to the people to eat," Elisha said. 2 Kings ch.4 v42

With Elisha the prophet of God. 'Give the barley to the people to eat'. He left it for the people to give it to the hundred men who were there. Instead of bringing the firstfruits of the new harvest to the false priests at Bethel and Dan (see 1 Kings ch.12 v28-31). Godly people in the northern kingdom may have contributed their offerings for the sustenance of the prophet Elisha and those associated with him. They looked on Elisha as the true representative of God rather than false prophets under king Jeroboam.

- - - - - - -

Despair, all you farmers! Wail, all you vine growers! Weep, because the wheat and barley—all the crops of the field—are ruined. Joel ch.1 v11 (NLT)

The prophet Joel was saying that the massive locust plague was coming, a severe drought was coming on Judah. He calls everyone to repent, to turn to the Lord. We don't know exactly when Joel was written. In the last book (see Revelation ch.9 v1-11), Satan was evil and he wants all people to suffer horribly. He manifested hostile, spiteful, vicious powers over mankind out of the abyss, the locusts appeared.

The barley and wheat were ruined in the book of Joel, all the crops of the field failed and it might be the same thought of the prophet's prophecy.

- - - - - - -

While everyone was sleeping, his enemy came and sowed weeds among the wheat, and went away. When the wheat sprouted and formed ears, then the weeds also appeared. Matthew ch.13 v25-26

It is the same in both the Old and New Testaments there is no real difference. When man sinned and turned against God and forgot him. All the troubles will come upon the earth (see Deuteronomy ch.31 v15-21). The weeds will appear due to man's sin (see Genesis ch.3 v18), because Adam and Eve went to the tree of the knowledge of good and evil, you (like them) took fruit for yourself to be like God.

Many disasters and difficulties will come upon them, and on that day, they will ask, "Have not these disasters come upon us because our God is not with us?" Deuteronomy ch.31 v17

Do you not realise that all the waste and burdensome events have come upon us because all men and women sinned? The rivers are polluted, plastics are everywhere, the world is littered with waste. Satan is looking very pleased with himself, he likes men to try to get things changed. The authorities are not willing to pursue that because of the thought of money, but they don't admit it.

They protestors are focused on the waste but not on God. They concentrated not on sin to make things better for all men.

- - - - - - -

So they gathered them and filled twelve baskets with the pieces of the five barley loaves left over by those who had eaten. John ch.6 v13

Jesus feeds the five thousand. He went up to a mountain and saw a great crowd coming toward him because they saw the miraculous signs he did. He said to one of his disciples, "Where shall we buy bread for these people to eat?" He said this because he had in mind what he was going to achieve (see John ch.6 v6).

After they had finished the meal, the disciples gathered all the bread left over. The bread consisted of five barley loaves and two small tiny fish. Not enough for the multitude that was gathered round him, all expecting Jesus to feed them. There was even barley bread left over, 12 baskets full. Did you know that the baskets were empty when they sat down to eat? Jesus did more than feed the crowd and he left the baskets there to feed the birds.

Simon, Simon, Satan was asked to sift you as wheat. But I have prayed for you, Simon, that your faith may not fail. And when you have turned back, strengthen your brothers. Luke ch.22 v31-32

At the end of his life on earth, Jesus said to Peter, 'Satan has arranged for you to be shaken and trampled like wheat.' What does it mean?

The grain was separated from the husk by threshing or beating with a heavy flail. To separate the wheat from the stalk. It involved a lot of work, flogging it to try to remove the good seed. The husk, the remainder will fly away in the wind. Peter will face this but his faith will not fail. It started with Jesus being arrested and Peter was there at his previous trial. The three people all were subject to Satan's enticement and asked Peter if he was one of them. Peter denied it and slowly Peter's work began to fail. At the end he went outside and cried. He wept bitterly but his faith in Jesus did not fail.

There is no doubt that Satan will try to finish off the people of God, even the elect (see Matthew ch.24 v22). He would punish, persecuted them and put them to death. You will be hated by all nations because of me (see Matthew ch.24 v9). Peter was the one who stood out when Jesus was glorified (see Acts ch.1 v15). His faith was enough to shake off the devil. He was the person whom Satan turned to, trying to stop the church forming.

- - - - - - -

And what you put in the ground is not the plant that will grow, but only a bare seed of wheat or whatever you are planting. Then God gives it the new body he wants it to have. 1 Corinthians ch.15 v37-38 (NLT)

The strong wheat will still be there at the end. God's promise to Noah still stands (see Genesis ch.9 v9). Nothing can spoil the wheat from giving a harvest for all the people, both in Jerusalem after Jesus was glorified and eventually the whole world.

After we die God decides what body we should have. One seed of wheat it is a small seed, but God makes it special, for he has a body that we can't know about while here on this earth. We will have to wait and see.

DOUBT

Doubt is unsure or hesitant, doubt is to get worried.

And he recognised it and said, "It is my son's tunic. A wild beast has devoured him. Without doubt Joseph is torn to pieces." Then Jacob tore his clothes, put sackcloth on his waist, and mourned for his son many days. Genesis ch.37 v33-34 (NKJV)

Jacob had twelve sons (see Genesis ch.35 v22), he had four wives two of which were maidservants of Leah and Rachel, Bilhah and Zilpah (see Genesis ch.35 v23-26), one daughter (see Genesis ch.34 v1).

Joseph was seventeen, he was the eleventh son that Jacob had conceived with Rachel (see Genesis ch.30 v22-24). He was chosen by his father and presented with a richly ornamental coat (see Genesis ch.37 v3). The brothers hated him. Why?

> He gave a bad report about his brothers.
> His father doted on him as special and loved him.
> He had two special dreams and he told his brothers.
> The brothers couldn't speak a kind word for him.

While they were looking after their sheep away in Dothan, the brothers sold him to the Midianite traders to take him to Egypt. It was a very nasty business but they thought that Joseph was dead. They took Joseph's coat, slaughtered a goat and dipped it in the blood. There was no doubt that Joseph had been slain when they arrived back at their home. Jacob mourned for Joseph for many days, but he refused to be comforted. Doubt was always there.

- - - - - - -

You will live in constant suspense; filled with dread both night and day, never sure of your life. In the morning you will say, "If it were evening!" and in the evening, "If it were morning!" - because of the terror that will fill your heart and the sights that your eyes will see. Deuteronomy ch.28 v66-67

The curses for disobedience when Israel did not obey the Lord their God (see Deuteronomy ch.28 v15). There was much to be said about what will happen in the city, in the country, cursed when you go in and out (see Deuteronomy ch.28 v16-68). But you will live in constant suspense because of the terror that will fill your heart and what you will see with your eyes. You can remember what you saw even up to the days of your death, the guilt will be there for a long while.

This is the same as today, where grown men and women were over-filled with uncertainty and anxiety. They can't see what will happen, it will flood their minds and fix their souls on what will be done. It is anticipation for what will occur when their children mature and get old. This is true when you are filled with sin and don't obey the Lord your God. The heart gets hard and fixed in time so the conscience doesn't worry you; you forget about what will happen.

- - - - - - -

Immediately Jesus reached out his hand and caught him. "You of little faith," he said, "Why did you doubt." Matthew ch.14 v31

Jesus reaches out his hand to guide Peter who was sinking in the water. The water was buffeted by the waves, it was cold and the wind was blowing fiercely. Peter started out walking on the water but he didn't finish. He saw the wind and was afraid and he was beginning to sink down in the water (see Mathew ch.14 v29-30). Jesus said, 'Why did you doubt?'. He started out, it was fine and he fixed his eyes on Jesus who was walking on the sea. But he forgot and noticed the wind and the waves so he started to sink in the sea.

Doubt is a present cause of distrust while we start on life's journey. We are confident that the Lord will hold us up, but looking around we see problems and difficulties that makes us afraid. Concentrate solely on Jesus and he will make the way easier. It doesn't mean that the problems will go away and the Holy Spirit will enter your mind and tell you what you should be doing.

Jesus replied, "I tell you the truth, if you have faith and do not doubt, not only can you do what was done to the fig-tree, but also you can say to this mountain, Go, throw yourself into the sea, and it will be done." Matthew ch.21 v21

If you have faith and do not doubt. The reason is we don't have faith enough to trust Jesus on what he has in mind for us to do. We hesitate and look around even backwards to where we started out. When you face persecution or suffering, when the devil begins to shake you, trust in Jesus and he will guide you in what you have to face.

Come to me, all you who are weary and burdened, and I will give you rest. Take my joke upon you and learn from me, for I am gentle and humble in heart, and you will find rest for your souls. For my yoke is easy and my burden is light. Matthew ch.11 v28-30

When you come to Jesus and take his burden upon you surprisingly his burden is light. But you have to take his burden upon you and don't think this is not for me.

Yoke: it is taking about something that joins together, it is part of a garment that fits the shoulders, a bond, a mark of servitude. This is what Jesus means by going together with him and keeping up with him, what ever the consequences. Whether we pass or fail, we are still with him. Doubt is not one word we should be using.

- - - - - - -

Jesus walked in the temple, in Solomon's porch. Then the Jews surrounded Him and said to Him, "How long do You keep us in doubt? If You are the Christ, tell us plainly." John ch.10 v23-24 (NKJV)

It is the unbelief of the Jews that surrounds this passage in Scripture. They don't understand what Jesus was doing. His miracles, his teaching, his healing and still they can't understand it, nor figure it out. Because their minds are filled with sin.

The mind of sinful man is death, but the mind controlled by the Spirit if life and peace; the sinful mind is hostile to God. It does not submit to God's law, nor can it do so. Those controlled by the sinful nature cannot please God. Romans ch.8 v6-8

Again, they tried to seize him, but he escaped their grasp. John ch.10 v39

The unbelief of the Jews, the chief priests and the Sanhedrin makes his death on the cross simply beyond belief. He went willingly in the Old Testament to offer himself as a sacrifice for us all. That is why he died and rose again.

Doubt makes unbelievers cold and hard. They couldn't see what God had achieved. They are blinded by Satan.

- - - - - - -

For our sakes, no doubt, this is written, that he who plows should plow in hope, and he who threshes in hope should be partaker of his hope. 1 Corinthians ch.9 v10 (NKJV)

The apostle Paul had lots of problems with the Corinth believers. I am not surprised because this was a lawless and dreadful place. It was not a university place like Athens, but it was characterised by Greek culture. The temple of Aphrodite goddess of love and was open for unbridled immorality. At one time one thousand sacred prostitutes served the temple.

So Paul stayed for one year and a half teaching them the word of God. The Jews made a concentrated attack on Paul (see Acts ch.18 v11-12). They didn't like what he said. He who sows, should sow in hope but the harvest will come. This is what doubt brings. If you didn't sow like Paul did and you failed to reap the rewards.

- - - - - - -

So when the natives saw the creature hanging from his hand, they said to one another, "No doubt this man is a murderer, whom, though he has escaped the sea, yet justice does not allow to live." Acts ch.28 v4 (NKJV)

The apostle Paul was on a journey to Rome to see the Caesar Nero; he was a prisoner under the Roman Empire. He had gone around Asia Minor going into Greece had a lot of Gentiles who were coming to the Lord. Some Jews from the province of Asia in Jerusalem stirred up the crowd and attacked Paul saying, 'This man has brought Greeks into the temple area'. This was a fabrication (see Acts ch.21 v29). So Paul was in chains and was ordered to appear before the governor, he eventually appealed to Caesar.

While he was on his making his way to Italy but the ship was in a storm and was broken up with the waves (see Acts ch.27 v1- ch.28 v1). When they were eventually rescued it was wet and cold and they built a fire to get warm. A viper driven out by the heat fastened on to Paul's hand. The islanders were convinced this man was a murderer and has escaped from the sea. Doubt thought he was suspect and they were beginning to think that he was one of them. Paul shook of the viper into the fire and suffered no harm so they changed their minds and thought him a god.

You can't reason with doubt.

DREAD

Dread is a great fear to feel anxiety or nervousness.

Beginning today I will make people throughout the earth terrified because of you. When they hear reports about you, they will tremble with dread and fear. Deuteronomy ch.2 v25 (NLT)

When the Israelites journeyed through the wasteland in the Wilderness of Paran. Most of the people had died in the desert. The children had to face the coming battle through Edom and Moab to go into the Promised Land (see Numbers ch.14 v22-23). They finally arrived at the River Jordan. They were frightened and unprepared for the fight to overthrow Canaan. God said, 'Don't worry I will protect you'. The enemy would hear the reports of the conflict and melt away because God will fight against them.

Each time the Lord will put the dread of you on all the nations.

No one will be able to stand against you, for the Lord your God will cause the people to fear and dread you, as he promised, wherever you go in the whole land. Deuteronomy ch.11 v25 (NLT)

Each man will not be able to stand against you. Why? The Lord your God has promised the Israelites. He will put the terror and dread of you. Wherever you go into the whole of the Promised Land. He will protect and care for you, as you go, he will cause the enemy to melt away.

This was a noticeable change for the people living in Canaan. Why did he do it? (see Deuteronomy ch.9 v1-6)

You are going to enter and dispossess the nations.
Nations greater and stronger than the Israelites.
God will destroy and subdue them
Because it is the wickedness of these nations.
They were using idols and magic.
Not because of the righteousness of Israel.

The Canaanites had detestable practices that is why God would wipe them out (see Deuteronomy ch.18 v9-13).

- - - - - - -

I am innocent, but it makes no difference to me—I despise my life. Job ch.9 v21 (NLT)

Everyone had sinned because he came from Adam and Eve, the penalty was that of death (see Genesis ch.3 v19). We die as we get old and we can't do anything about it. We have treatments, body parts, new teeth, hair replacements and the rest. But we still get old, worn out and fragile. As the years go on, we forget, each day seems to be fine. Then the years follow on, we fall asleep in the day time, we forget the past, because all our days are numbered by God. He knows the day we die.

Job was presented with painful sores over his body due to Satan's attempt to force him to reject God (see Job ch.2 v7). He understood that he was going to die from his illness (see Job ch.3 v21-22). This dread will still be there we know that there is a judgement, where everybody will come to the great white throne for their time on earth. This is true as we get old or have a disease which is unfortunately terminal. We don't know when the time will come, so be ready and don't delay.

- - - - - - -

Do not dread the disease that stalks in darkness, nor the disaster that strikes at midday. Though a thousand fall at your side, though ten thousand are dying around you, these evils will not touch you. Just open your eyes, and see how the wicked are punished. Psalm ch.91 v6-8 (NLT)

Just consider what God thinks. He regards and watches human life. He sees about the things of life, the flowers in the garden and the animals and the birds but the people on earth do not fear him, or even trust him. They are only interested in holding banners and shouting loud enough making a point to what they think should be done. They don't think about the evil who sin.

There are two things that we must be sure of: The righteous and the wicked or the good and the bad. If they don't consider God, or follow his path, the fruits of his purpose. Stampede over the ground, ignoring the authorities (see Roman ch.13 v1-5) are they sure they are bad and evil? The authorities are instituted by God, not by ourselves. We have a duty to protect them. Better to concentrate on what Jesus is planning to do for the church, there is a way that we must go and give of ourselves to preach and teach what Jesus has done (see Matthew ch.28 v18-20). This is what we should be doing, going out to reach the dread of those who are lost.

Do not call conspiracy everything that these people call conspiracy; do not fear what they fear, and do not dread it. The Lord Almighty is the one you are to regard as holy, he is the one you are to fear, he is the one you are to dread. Isaiah ch.8 v12-13

Do not call conspiracy what everyone thinks should be done. Think about what should be done to the Lord Almighty? He is the one who is holy. He is the one you should fear. He is the one you should dread. Don't get caught up in the conspiracy what other people think it is important. There are more important questions that we should be doing (see Matthew ch.6 v25-34). You will be side-tracked from what you should be carrying out.

The apostle Paul acted differently from what the others were doing. He was only doing his duty, preach the gospel to everyone even the Jews and Gentiles. He understood that the church in Corinth had problems, this is why he wrote to Corinth, but he maintained that the word of God should be taught. This is what we should dread, the coming fear of the Lord.

- - - - - - -

Yet you have forgotten the Lord, your Creator, the one who stretched out the sky like a canopy and laid the foundations of the earth. Will you remain in constant dread of human oppressors? Will you continue to fear the anger of your enemies? Where is their fury and anger now? It is gone! Isaiah ch.51 v13 (NLT)

Yet you have forgotten the creator of the world who made even you! You have the stars to remind you of the distance that God travels. A stone you can pick up on the beach we can't make even that with all the computers and machines. The birds of the air they have all specked colours and patterns, each one is different. Do you think that man has engineered that? Look around you see the waves coming up the shore line. The waves flow evenly for the high tide and low tide coupled with the moon that passes by. God created the moon but we didn't.

God sees and watches over mankind (see Psalm ch.121). He will also watch you and sees what you are doing. He knows when you get up and go to bed, he knows about your thinking which you don't mention to anyone else. Do you think he doesn't know about the dread of your enemies?

- - - - - - -

Therefore, the anger of the Lord had fallen on Judah and Jerusalem; he has made them an object of dread and horror and scorn, as you can see with your own eyes. 2 Chronicles ch.29 v8

When the Israelites were in the Promised Land. They still failed to do what God's instructions and commands had told them to do. They still had idols (see Deuteronomy ch.13) and they had magic and potions (see 2 Kings ch.21 v1-16). It was the same as the nations behaved before God gave them the land. They broke the Ten Commandments that God had given them (see Exodus ch.20 v1-17).

They were pitiful people, so the prophet Jeremiah who wrote Kings and Chronicles said they were, 'An object of dread and horror'. King Manasseh filled Jerusalem with trouble and he managed to get the temple of the Lord filled with altars to all the starry hosts. The people didn't listen to what God had said, they ignored him and failed to do what he had planned. Do you think of Israel and Judah sent away to slavery under the exiled people? If God had done that the people he chose, what about you? Do you think that God will be different? He is the same God and he will carry out his intention for this whole earth (see 2 Peter ch.3 v10). He will decide to put the dread of what he has planned.

EARTH AND HEAVENS

Earth is the substance in which plants are made. The heavens are the vault of sky overhanging the earth.

In the beginning God created the heavens and the earth. Now the earth was formless and empty, darkness was over the surface of the deep. Genesis ch.1 v1-2

God created the heavens and the earth out of nothing. Now the earth was a deep ocean and darkness covered the face of the earth. Modern scholars have decided that it was wrong and impossible. They think that it was a 'big bang' but they failed to realise that the earth was covered with oceans and not a mighty explosion, it was deep water and very cold. They do not understand the Almighty, holy and fearsome God. They are not willing to let him decide what will happen in the past. This is the same reason as all of the group of demonstrators think that the world is going to end. They do not understand what God has patiently explained in the Bible:

God said, "This is the sign of my covenant I am making between me and you and every living creature with you, a covenant for all the generations to come: I have set my rainbow in the clouds and it will be sign of the covenant between me and the earth." Genesis ch.9 v12-13

It is a reminder of God promise to us for all the generations to come and included all the animals. But the sky was different, the colours were not as it were today and the rainbow did not appear. The colours of the sky were changed by God as a sign of his covenant.

When you see the rainbow, think about what God has told you because the rainbow marks God's present with you even now. We know that the rainbow is coloured by the rain passing though the sun, but it wasn't like that before Noah and the flood. God altered it, even man is simple, he thinks that with glass he can make the rainbow appear. But he has forgotten the arc of the rainbow when the sun comes out, when it is pouring rain and only one rainbow appears in the sky and it is the same place.

- - - - - - -

So you may know that there is no-one like me (God) in all the earth. Exodus ch.9 v14

This is why when we think about God, we are only a small part of his creation (see Job ch.38 - ch.39). God made all of it, suddenly it was there:

The earth's underpin foundations.

The sea behind the shut doors.

The morning comes each day as the world rotates.

The gates of death will be there, and

The abode of light.

The storehouses of snow.

The water is there constantly.

The stars that shine brightly.

The clouds that form in the sky.

The lightning bolts and thunder, and

The animals needed to be fed.

Consider the lightning, man did not understand it. For all the weather producers and consultants are not sure of what it is. How could such power come from so little clouds? Most of the lightning is in the air, only a small amount falls to the ground. Forked, sheet or streaking lightning depending on how far away when you gazed up at the sky. Each day the lightning flashes around the world; it is only one amazing thing about God's power and might.

We don't even know about all of the creation, suddenly we find another creature that we are not sure if what it is called. We look it up in the animal books and there are no facts about it. We are not surprised that the creation is a majestic act of God. He shows us what he can do. No one maps the deep oceans, we have underwater machines with lights that feebly shine out in the darkness, but it is a mystery to us. We are not sure if the ships that have sunk over the years, we are still searching for it.

The sinful mind is hostile to God. It does not submit to God's law, nor can it do so. Those controlled by the sinful nature cannot please God. Romans ch.8 v7-8

But the experts who publish books, the teachers and professors don't think that God made it. They forget and silence the Lord who made everyone. When a baby is born who manages it to form the breath that we have? When we die it is the same body that is old and infirm, where do we go when our body dies? The authorities don't know and they have a wide range of other options. The truth is 'the sinful mind is hostile to God' who made and created it.

But the Lord is in his holy Temple; the Lord still rules from heaven. He watches everyone closely, examining every person on earth. The Lord examines both the righteous and the wicked. He hates those who love violence. He will rain down blazing coals and burning sulphur on the wicked, punishing them with scorching winds. For the righteous Lord loves justice.

The virtuous will see his face. Psalm ch.11 v4-7 (NLT)

God is watching you, he watches everyone closely. To see if they are good or bad. When you get up, he sees you, even if its dark. When you are dressed, he observes you, when you go to work, he contemplates you. He has a mind when you are at work and when you get home, he keeps his eye on you. He notices you in the evening and views you when you go to bed. Every day he watches you, whether it is the weekend or not. To see if you respond to him. He notices that you respond to righteousness and justice. He writes it in his book every and each day. There's a lot of books that for the whole of your life. He looks into your heart and sees what you think. You might not say it, but he is aware of it (see Psalm ch.139).

God hates and detests those who love violence and aggression with mankind fighting.

- - - - - - -

In the beginning you laid the foundations of the earth, and the heavens are the work of your hands. They will perish, but you remain; they will wear out like a garment. Like clothing you will change them and they will be discarded. But you remain the same, and your years will never end. Psalm ch.102 v25-27

Trust in the Lord! He created all of it and the parts that man has not even seen. Man is only interested in what is on the surface of the earth not above and below from what is hidden from him. Nothing about heaven. Aeroplanes go into it, but they come down under gravity to go into the airport where mankind gets off and others gets on. They don't think about the heavens, where they are? He created it by the work of his hands.

God says, 'They will wear out like a garment'. You change your clothing every day? Do you consider how many clothes you wear for the whole of your life? Like garments they will be discarded: stars, trees, animals or even mankind. He replaces them, like trees. The seed will go into the ground and the shoots will appear. Then the tree will get bigger and after that, a whole tree. We don't have to do anything about it. The tree gets large over the years, the protestors come and go, with the message that we must do something. God promised Noah that while the earth remained all of the seasons will be there. Sowing and reaping, cold and hot, summer and winter. But he didn't say the earth will remain after the judgement while mankind face God. The Lord is there and will be there for ever. The earth will be destroyed by fire all of it and nobody would be left alive. Plants, animals, mankind will perish (see 2 Peter ch.3 v7).

When you give them your breath, life is created, and you renew the face of the earth. Psalm ch.104 v30 (NLT)

While God gave man breath, each one will go on looking and searching on the earth. What we do with it is open to question? Many people think that the rubbish on the earth, all the populations that grow on the earth will use up precious materials. If God removed the breath all life would cease. You can look at when the body dies. It will be the same but the breath has gone, mankind and the animals. Even the trees all the leaves are gone and the branches stand out during the winter. Eventually the branches weaken and the trees will fall and die.

Do you not realise? That God renewed the face of the earth. He didn't leave it alone, as the earth revolved around the sun. He renewed it. Why do you think that the plants grew in the first place? Each day, without any fuss, God mended and repaired the earth. In my garden two trees appeared one was a Grey Willow and the other was a Wild Cherry but I did not put them there. They grew up without me doing anything. God renewed my garden. He planted the seeds and they grew up into trees. Probably birds dropped the seeds.

Generations come and generations go, but the earth remains for ever. The sun rises and the sun sets, and hurries back to where it rises. The wind blows to the south and turns to the north; round and round it goes, ever returning on its course. All streams flow into the sea, yet the sea is never full. To the place the streams come from, there they return again. Ecclesiastes ch.1 v4-7

More people come and go, but the earth remains the same. You don't find it getting bigger or smaller, it is the identical size. The earth will revolve around the sun and will be there just as the time for mankind to face God in the judgement. We badly need the judgement to rectify the appalling problems on earth.

Round and round it goes: the sun, the wind, the rivers and the streams. The moon rotates around the earth. The point is that the earth is constant. Unchangeable, firm and which remains the same today while the variables may change accordingly with all the rubbish and materials that people use. We had deep mining, scarifying the hillside, coal and other minerals piled up and left to rot. We had planes and cars waiting to be used stretching over the valleys. But the earth will remain fixed and stable around the sun.

- - - - - - -

The earth will be completely laid waste and totally plundered. The Lord has spoken this word. Isaiah ch.24 v3

Due to the evil practices and violence that man has created, God in his holiness and justice will wipe the earth clean again. Noah only had eight people saved out of all the masses that were on the earth. No other relatives. He had been working on his boat for a very long time and many people would be mocking and laughing at him; but they were not saved. Eight people survived the flood, so what about now? Are we worse than those before the flood?

Many people thinks so and the time is approaching with all the violence on this earth. God in his holiness would wipe the earth again not flooding the earth but with fire. The earth is doomed to be wasted away. God told it to the prophet Isaiah who spoke about it 2,700 years ago! It will still come.

You know how to interpret the appearance of the earth and sky. How is it that you don't interpret this present time? Luke ch.12 v56

Most people find that the weather - the colours of the sun and the clouds bring sunshine and rain because they are obvious, look up at the sky. But most people can't decide what to do in this present time. The Bible is the key to finding out and many people don't read the Scriptures. God has made it plain what he is intending to do, but people don't like it. They dismiss the Bible as antiquated, old fashioned, been around for ages.

In the past, God in the Old Testament had many prophets that would go to the people but now in the New Testament it would be different. When Jesus came, he spoke the truth and the apostles carried on with his teaching. The prophets would be still here, but they are concentrating to avoid false teaching and prophecy which will come into the church. The only way is to read the Bible if you want to find out what God is saying. I don't mean going to church where a small section of the Bible is read that is primarily for Christians. But studying the Bible, on your own every day, to understand what God is saying to you personally.

- - - - - - -

It is easier for heaven and earth to disappear than for the smallest point of God's law to be overturned. Luke ch.16 v17 (NLT)

This is true for the smallest part of God's law to be overturned and misused. Jesus made it clear that the Old Testament is valid and is meaningful now. God had his reasons for the Ten Commandments (see Exodus ch.20 v1-17 and Deuteronomy ch.5 v6-21). This is why we had it twice in the Bible, it was important. It was God's covenant between him and us.

God's law is the right and just law to guide us in what we should be doing. This is why we have in England not the Statute Law but the Common Law to guide us and protect us.

There will be signs in the sun, moon and stars. On earth, nations will be in anguish and perplexity at the roaring and tossing of the sea. Men will faint from terror, apprehensive of what is coming on the world, for the heavenly bodies will be shaken. Luke ch.21 v25-26

When it is due on earth like the great tribulation (see Matthew ch.24 v3-31), Jesus will appear in the sky with power and great glory. Most of the inhabitants of the earth will mourn. Why did they mourn? Because their deeds were evil.

The increase of wickedness and evil, the love of many will grow cold. There will be famines and earthquakes in many places. Most of the believers will be hated and killed. False prophets will appear and perform great signs and wonders. This is because the earth will grow worse and man will cease to be satisfied and do evil things like idols and slavery and forget the God who made us.

The earth is the Lord's, and everything in it. 1 Corinthians ch.10 v26

Don't think that the earth is Satan's domain. He will be active and malicious and with his band of fallen angels. He will be looking out for all the believers to kill them. However, the earth is God's home, he would act with the right and proper ideas. Satan was forced to get out of heaven with his fallen angels but he was left on earth to deceive all mankind (see Job ch.1 v7 and Matthew ch.4 v8-9).

God created the earth and heavens, why should Satan take that away? Satan and his fallen angels were made by God. They eventually were punished in the lake of burning sulphur to be tormented day and night for ever (see Revelation ch.20 v10). Satan would lose all his powers and not get out, he would stay there forever.

- - - - - - -

Set you minds on things above, not on earthly things. Colossians ch.3 v2

What does it mean? The believer must concentrate on heavenly things (see Galatians ch.5 v22-23). Not on the sordid basic things: like adultery, idols to make, magic to control and murder people.

You can see what the newspapers and television think about that. Presenters, books, education and the social media they are full of earthly things. They are not suitable for spiritual things; like reading the Bible, going to church, speaking to people and singing spiritual songs. The responsibility for believers is looking for what is good, going forth to make treasures in heaven.

By the same word the present heavens and earth are reserved for fire, being kept for the day of judgement and destruction of ungodly men. 2 Peter ch.3 v7

When Jesus will return again and there is no doubt about it (see Acts ch.1 v9-11). He will begin to reign over the people on the earth, with faithfulness and justice. The apostle John saw that he would make war on the worthless people and destroy them (see Revelation ch.19 v11-21). The present heavens and earth will be 'reserved for fire'. Trashing any man-made equipment, buildings, roads, bridges and the rest. To take it back to the Garden of Eden where animals roamed freely and trees and plants grew up to cover the land (see Isaiah ch.11 v9).

Then I saw a new heaven and a new earth, for the first heaven and the first earth had passed away, and there was no longer any sea. Revelation ch.21 v1

Then the apostle John saw a new heaven and a new earth for the first ones would be gone. He saw there was no longer any sea. The sea means that the earth would not have any boundaries or nations with different languages. they could all meet, one with each other.

The Holy City combines the elements of Jerusalem, the temple and the Garden of Eden (see Revelation ch.21 v2). There the believers would be present to rejoice with God. They had been saved, by coming to the cross and believing on Jesus and carrying on with what he suggested. Not worrying about the persecution and suffering they had experienced while on earth that the believers had been made to do.

END

The end as the last point, termination or close.

O righteous God, who searches minds and hearts, bring to an end the violence of the wicked and make the righteous secure. Psalm ch.7 v9

God will separate the good from the bad, whatever the circumstances, whether you are rich or poor, young or old. He is certain to do it because he knows the minds and hearts of all the people. The violence of the wicked will ceases to be a factor on the earth, or giving animals a hard time.

God likes the plants and trees to form because he made them before he created mankind, who had the wicked and evil things to remain on the earth. It's a terrible place where man sought God; his mind was made up for all the killings that took place where people are unique and different, had their own gods that they serve. Particularly our own believers were merciless slain by people outside of them.

Let the rich of the earth feast and worship. Bow before him, all who are mortal, all whose lives will end as dust. Psalm ch.22 v29 (NLT)

As we come to the end of our life, we will be faced with going to the grave. Our lives will end as dust because Adam and Eve sinned against God. They exerted themselves above God's will. God did not intend for them to die, he made sure that mankind and animals could remain forever. Let the 'rich feast and worship' but they all will come to the judgement where God is supreme and is not frightened by the masses that come together.

- - - - - - -

Everyone will bow to the God and there are no exceptions or excuses.

He makes wars cease to the ends of the earth; he breaks the bow and shatters the spear, he burns the shields with fire. Psalm ch.46 v9

God is in control whereas man is prone to hatred, anger and even war. Mankind is only a small part of God's plan. The impact of war makes all the plants and trees destroyed and gone, man is determined to fight and control many lives with his plan. Widows, homeless-people, aliens would get in the way and be removed. Houses, bridges and roads were demolished. Mankind tries to make his weapons stronger than the enemy who would fight back against him.

God looks down and sees the situation. He decides to end all wars. But the rulers, generals and politicians don't see it that way, they think they have won. Looking back in history, nobody wins with fighting and war. Some people exert power over their neighbours, but the result is that all will die and be lost. The damage of war is inexcusable, man has to rebuild it again. It is pointless and a waste of energy. The fields would come again but the impact of the war makes it certain that people would be killed after the war is over, because of the horror of war and many people have appalling injuries. They last for ever until the end.

Then God said, 'The war is over and ended' (see Revelation ch.20 v9).

- - - - - - -

I will maintain my love to him for ever, and my covenant with him will never fail. I will establish his line for ever, his throne as long as the heavens endure. Psalm ch.89 v28-29

Do you wonder what God is doing now? God is patient, kind, holy and righteous. He has made a commitment that his love will last for ever while the heavens last. Regardless of the protestors who scream and shout and make life unbearable for the rest. His throne will be there after the world is judged. People think that God isn't interested in people they think that God has gone away, but he hasn't (see Psalm ch.14).

But God is watching carefully. God considers our hearts to see if any understand him and see what he does. He sent his son Jesus to rescue us from sin (see John ch.3 v16-17) and we can't do it for ourselves. Our lives are controlled by Satan. Who likes men and women to fight between themselves? God decides what will happen, not Satan. The end is very close and near.

- - - - - - -

He has made everything beautiful in its time. He has also set eternity in the hearts of men; yet they cannot fathom what God has done from beginning to end. Ecclesiastes ch.3 v11

King Solomon had wisdom that came from God (see 1 Kings ch.3 v12). He understood that God had created everything beautiful, he also knew that mankind could not understand God's plan.

God plan was there in the beginning and is there in the end. Satan is a nuisance, he made man think that God was not interested in people. His fallen angels tried hard to get men away from God. But it is not working as Satan would have it. God eventually would remove Satan and his fallen angels in the battle of Armegeddon (see Revelation ch.20 v7-10), but God is still waiting for those who might come to be saved. It might be for you.

- - - - - - -

Naked a man comes from his mother's womb, and as he comes, so he departs. He takes nothing from his labour that he can carry in his hand. Ecclesiastes ch.5 v15

Man could arrive without any clothes and no wealth, eventually they would die with nothing, not even any riches that they would make on earth. King Solomon knew it was pointless. He will take nothing from his labour on this world, anybody can profit from his work while he lived. Even the rich man when he dies will take nothing with him. The Egyptians didn't know or understand that. The Pharaoh had gold treasures from the land where he lived and buried them into the pyramids when he died. Some were taken by thieves, but some were left behind.

The end is when our soul is removed by God to go to Hades and then wait until the judgement and this will come soon.

- - - - - - -

All men will hate you because of me, but he who stands firm to the end will be saved. Matthew ch.10 v22

Jesus came to earth to save the world through his sacrifice for himself. He died for sins once, to bring you to God (see 1 Peter ch.3 v18). Each person could not go to heaven because God is holy and just and would never let any sin come before him. Jesus said, 'All men will hate you because of me'. He was rejected by men who should have known better, who had the Mosaic Law which read by the Jews in the the synagogues.

The end of this world is when you die. You will have to make a choice whether you want to go to heaven or not?

As the weeds are pulled up and burned in the fire, so it will be at the end of the age. Matthew ch.13 v40

There are two roads that we are on. One such road that leads to destruction and many enter through it. The other road leads to life. But it is narrow and only a few find it (see Matthew ch.7 v13-14). At the end of the age in Hades and after the judgement the one road leads to hell. The other road is narrow and twisted and many people miss it. It leads to Jesus and his cross. Most people take the broad road. They live it up, lively parties, houses, watching television and brand new cars. They offer idols rather than seeking God.

These things happened to them as examples for us. They were written down to warn us who live at the end of the age. If you think you are standing strong, be careful not to fall. 1 Corinthians ch.10 v11-12 (NLT)

Be strong and don't let the message fail because you don't understand. The Bible is clear, the Scriptures are written down for us. It is only for you and you will have to decide whether you can come to Jesus and tell him how sorry you are. Your parents can't decide for you, nor can your friends. Even going to church then the vicar tells you, 'You will have to decide on your own'. We don't know when you might be killed, an accident, a fatal occasion or later in life.

- - - - - - -

For you have been born again, but not to a life that will quickly end. Your new life will last forever because it comes from the eternal, living word of God. As the Scriptures say, "People are like grass; their beauty is like a flower in the field. The grass withers and the flower fades. But the word of the Lord remains forever." 1 Peter ch.1 v23-25 (NLT)

The new birth only occurs through the direct action of the Holy Spirit (see Titus ch.3 v5), but the word of God also plays an important role (see James ch.1 v22). For it presents the gospel to the sinner and calls on him to repent and believe in Jesus.

Repent: to be sorry for your sins, to change from the past evil or misconduct; it means changing your mind.

Believe: to regard as true and to be firmly convinced that Jesus is the way.

'The word of God reigns forever' but you will not a have another chance. The flower fades but the end is very close and near. This is the time to do it!

FEAR

The fear as a painful emotion by the thought of danger.

All the animals of the earth, all the birds of the sky, all the small animals that scurry along the ground, and all the fish in the sea will look on you with fear and terror. I have placed them in your power. Genesis ch.9 v2 (NLT)

God has made mankind over all the animals, birds, fish to be superior to them and placed under man's power. They will look on you with fear and terror, but with kindness they will approach you. God selected man and woman to have control over all his nature; this was a great, immense situation. Each man had a duty to look after the animals (see Genesis ch.1 v28), he was responsible to care for them and feed them.

Adam was in charge of, he was close to God himself and could see him and hear him (see Genesis ch.3 v8-9). All animals respected and feared man. It was a harmony that God had selected and would live forever. But sin came in to the world and it was all changed immediately. Animals fought against each other and they became fearful of other dangers in their lives.

- - - - - - -

When the people saw the thunder and lightning and heard the trumpet and saw the mountain in smoke, they trembled with fear. They stayed at a distance. Exodus ch.20 v18

They trembled with fear and didn't look to the mountain where God was. Do not think that God's display of his majesty is intended to fill you with fear? But he controls all the world and he hates all of the sin that man does. The thunder, lightning and the trumpet and saw the mountain covered with smoke billowing around. If there is a volcano then up from the ground will come the eruption where molten rock forms onto the surface, and where will it go with the Israelites standing round the mountain?

There they had a vision of God:

> There was thunder directly above them.
> There was lightning flashing around the people.
> There was smoke around the mountain.
> There was a thick cloud over the mountain.
> There was the trumpet blasting out where God was, and
> The whole mountain trembled violently.

Never forget the day when you stood before the Lord your God at Mount Sinai, where he told me, 'Summon the people before me, and I will personally instruct them. Then they will learn to fear me as long as they live, and they will teach their children to fear me also.' Deuteronomy ch.4 v10-11 (NLT)

The people were rightly terrified and afraid. Nobody will want to go up and see God, so Moses went up to the top of the mountain (see Exodus ch.19 v20; ch.20 v21). He understood that God was creating for his Israelites the fear and terror of God. They will learn what God has instructed them to do, not just them, but the children after them.

No wonder our hearts have melted in fear! No one has the courage to fight after hearing such things. For the Lord your God is the supreme God of the heavens above and the earth below. Joshua ch.2 v11 (NLT)

'No one has the courage to face God'. Sadly, at the great while throne we will be there in front of God to be judged. To fear him and only him.

The Israelites failed to do what God had intended. Their Israelite descendants didn't bother with what God had done while on Mount Sinai. But they all knew about it and the Mosaic Law was written down for them. As the time goes on, we tend to forget God in his majesty, it was a distant past. The children tend to overlook God, but he will definitely remember, he watches everyone closely and he writes it in his book.

- - - - - - -

When the Israelites had come into the Promised Land, they had the city of Jericho to fight. Across the River Jordan which was in flood, the waters reached across the land where they were (see Joshua ch.3 v15). Jericho was a powerful enemy. It had double walls around the city and the gates were shut up tightly (see Joshua ch.6 v1). Jericho means the 'moon city', God was destroying not only a city but the whole area for the purpose of the false religion of the Canaanites.

Two spies went out from the Israelites to cover the Promised Land. Rahab the prostitute in Jericho took them in and hid them. She agreed that no-one could fight Israel for the Lord God is with your people. Her thoughts were 'melted in fear' of what the Israelites could and would do (see Joshua ch.6 v25).

- - - - - - -

The eyes of the Lord are on those who fear him, on those whose hope is in his unfailing love, to deliver them from death and keep them alive in famine. Psalm ch.33 v18-19

The Lord our God who created us. Even our minds, eyes, hearing and our feelings. It is important that we fear and respect the Lord our God. He arranges us in families to guide us, schools and streets where we live, the jobs we go to.

The Lord guides us during the famine and the earthquake. But he is God and he watches us to see how we are doing.

The angel of the Lord encamps around those who fear him, and he delivers them. Psalm ch.34 v7

Those who are good, the angel of the Lord protects them and he arranges a barrier around those to protect them (see Job ch.1 v10). Nothing that Satan can do will withstand the 'hedge' that the Lord has put around us without God giving permission.

I am not saying that on earth that we are given protection (see Matthew ch.24 v9), but the work of the believers has to stand up to the devil and he will fight hard to bring you down (see Hebrews ch.11 v35-38). Jesus prayed to his Father that 'you will protect them from the evil one' (see John ch.17 v15).

The angel of the Lord will protect us and encamps around us; if we fear and respect God.

- - - - - - -

Therefore, we will not fear, though the earth gives way and the mountains fall into the heart of the sea, though its waters roar and foam and the mountains quake with their surging. Psalm ch.46 v2-3

We are strong, the believer will not fear while the body of the earth is shaken:

> The earth gives way completely.
> The mountains fall into the sea.
> The sea is more violent than ever.
> The mountains shake with their troubles.

No, we do not fear, because the Lord has made a promise that we are protected while here in earth. Remember back in the book of Genesis, God said he would never destroy all living creatures including mankind? (see Genesis ch.8 v21).

Who knows the power of your anger? For your wrath is as great as the fear that is due to you. Psalm ch.90 v11

The power, supremacy and might of God. Who knows the power of your anger? He did to the Canaanite tribes when the Israelites fought against them, he destroyed them in the Promised Land. Later, Israel and Judah were exiled because they didn't do as God commanded. They were taken away as captives before the Assyrian Empire and the Babylonian Empire, hundreds of miles away. Who knows the strength of God?

The book of Lamentations shares the overwhelming state of loss that accompanied the destruction of Jerusalem, the city, temple and ritual in about 580 BC. All the treasures gone and the walls broken down (see 2 Chronicles ch.36 v17-19). The fear of God, that might come true if you don't repent of your sins.

- - - - - - -

As a father has compassion on his children, so the Lord has compassion on those who fear him. Psalm ch.103 v13

God is patient and kind and loves every single person. Remember, there were many people all around on the earth? God thinks of you when your parents had intercourse (see Psalm ch.51 v5). The Lord made you as he intended. Some are rich and some are poor, some have properties and some don't, some have every kind of luxury, some go out and take water from the river where they don't even have running water.

God created you as he thought best and we don't really understand it. God knew what he was doing and Jesus came into the world totally as a stranger, his parents were not married. There was a decree in the Roman world and everyone crowded to register where he was born. Mary went to Jerusalem on a donkey and was not a fit place at all for a pregnant woman. There was no room for the baby in the inn and Jesus was placed in a manger with the animals.

Joseph his father died in his early years. He understood what it was like, to be poor and have nothing of value. But God loved him and he was not fearful (see Luke ch.2 v40).

They do not fear bad news; they confidently trust the Lord to care for them. They are confident and fearless and can face their foes triumphantly. They share freely and give generously to those in need. Their good deeds will be remembered forever. Psalm ch.112 v7-9 (NLT)

They confidently trust that the Lord would care for them. They share out of their generosity with those in need. This is what the Lord requires of you. Jesus hadn't a home while he was going round the people (see Matthew ch.8 v20), he didn't have any money (see Matthew ch.17 v27), his clothing was indeed frugal (see John ch.19 v23-24) and the women cared for his needs (see Mark ch.15 v41).

The believers confidently trust in the Lord to help them but they are not fearful because God will hold them up.

- - - - - - -

The Lord is for me, so I will have no fear. What can mere people do to me? Yes, the Lord is for me; he will help me. I will look in triumph at those who hate me. It is better to take refuge in the Lord than to trust in people. It is better to take refuge in the Lord than to trust in princes. Psalm ch.118 v6-9 (NLT)

Many believers will still go out preaching the gospel of Christ, whereas some will be persecuted and will suffer the consequences. Some will go out as missionaries and some as preachers of the kingdom of God. We all will have a job to do. The Lord Jesus is with you, the Holy Spirit is on you, why should we fear, what will come?

I am losing all hope; I am paralysed with fear. I remember the days of old.
I ponder all your great works and think about what you have done. Psalm ch.143 v4-5 (NLT)

King David writes this Psalm as a prayer for deliverance from his enemies and for God's help. He starts his prayer with his own failings because he was aware the God might not listen to him. He knows that God is kind and would help him to get over his troubles.

It is a start where God might in the old days have great miracles like getting Israel out of Egypt. God is unchanged, he is the same yesterday and today. He watches over you, he might not give you a miraculous sign. He expects you to do it on your own, but with his help. Fear is common where you might not have a comfortable life and starting out with God's help. King David's reign ended with his boy Solomon, he gave this charge to his son, 'Be strong and walk with God' (see 1 Kings ch.2 v2-4). He reigned for over forty years (see 1 Chronicles ch.29 v27).

40 years and still king David reigned but he died at a good old age having enjoyed good life. But the Psalms are not fearful, king David enjoyed being with God whom he served day and night.

- - - - - - -

Since they hated knowledge and did not choose to fear the Lord, since they would not accept my advice and spurned my rebuke. Proverbs ch.1 v29-30.

The Israelites hated knowledge, they did not fear the Lord, they refused his advice and spurned his rebuke. King Solomon knew in his heart that his people would not trust the Lord. Even Moses understood that when he was old (see Deuteronomy ch.31 v27). Sin is always there, sin is what takes you away from God (see Romans ch.7 v19-20). The Israelites did not fear the Lord. It was a failing that most people have (see Romans ch.8 v7-8).

Then you will understand the fear of the Lord and find the knowledge of God. For the Lord gives wisdom, and from his mouth comes knowledge and understanding. Proverbs ch.2 v5-6

King Solomon would know the fear of the Lord. So what is the truth? It is based on wisdom, it requires knowledge and leads to understanding. Even king Solomon failed to keep the Lord's commands, but his wives turned his heart astray (see 1 Kings ch.11 v4-8). He loved many foreign wives. He failed to do as the Lord instructed him (see Deuteronomy ch.17 v17).

The fear of the Lord will do that for you. The knowledge of God involves knowing God and understanding what he has taught us.

- - - - - - -

Every arm is paralysed with fear. Every heart melts, and people are terrified. Pangs of anguish grip them, like those of a woman in labour. They look helplessly at one another, their faces aflame with fear. For see, the day of the Lord is coming—the terrible day of his fury and fierce anger. The land will be made desolate, and all the sinners destroyed with it. Isaiah ch.13 v7-9 (NLT)

The prophets often compare the suffering of judgement and war with the pain and anguish that frequently accompanies childbirth. It is not the fear that many people think that the world will end if we don't do something about it; but it is the 'day of the Lord'.

What will happen? When will it arrive? It is coming soon that terrible day. God's fury and fierce anger will be evident. The land will be made desolate and bare. The sinners and animals destroyed within it. (see Isaiah ch.13 v10-13):

The stars in heaven will not show their light.
The sun and moon will be silent.
The heaven and earth will shake.

It is an Old Testament prophecy, it would be about 3000 years ago. This is not new or uncertain, God emphasised it in the Bible. Due to the intensity of evil in the world, God's devastating curse will burn up the earth's inhabitants. This is truly fear.

They will eat their food in anxiety and drink their water in despair, for their land will be stripped of everything in it because of the violence of all who live there. Ezekiel ch.12 v19

In the prophet Ezekiel time, the land of Judah including Jerusalem, was under the power of King Nebuchadnezzar of Babylon. Who came to eliminate the people of Israel? To be hounded and exiled away from the Promised Land. The land of Palestine was broken up Israel were marched away by the Assyrian Empire who came first before the Babylonians.

But it will be true even when the 'day of the Lord' will come. Think about it:

They will eat their food in anxiety.
They will drink their water in despair.
The land will be stripped of everything.
The violence of the people there.

In the end when God had given the plagues to the people they still did not repent of their evil ways (see Revelation ch.16 v9-11). They cursed the God of heaven for their suffering. They understood that it was God who had done it, but they didn't repent for their sins.

- - - - - - -

For God has not given us a spirit of fear and timidity, but of power, love, and self-discipline. 2 Timothy ch.1 v7 (NLT)

God doesn't want us to be fearful or afraid of the Lord. He has given us the Holy Spirit not to fear, but be able to respond completely to what is about to happen.

The harvest is plentiful but the workers are few. Ask the Lord of the harvest, therefore, to send out workers into his harvest field. Matthew ch.9 v37-38

He wants us to go out without timidity, but of power, love and self-discipline. The workers will have to be strong but he has given us the Holy Spirit to enable us to go. Not in the churches, but out in the streets. Where we go from the many people from the young to the old, rulers and the crowd, rich and poor will hear the gospel (see Matthew ch.3 v1-2).

There is no fear in love. But perfect love drives out fear, because fear has to do with punishment. The one who fears is not made perfect in love. 1 John ch.4 v18

The fact that we are like Jesus is a sign that God who is love, lives in us. We may have confidence on the day of judgement that we are saved. There is no fear of God's judgement, because genuine love proves and has evidence that we are saved.

Perfect love drives out all fear that is what makes us bold to go out.

FIRE

Fire that it is a mass of burning matter and includes flames.

Then the Lord rained down burning sulphur on Sodom and Gomorrah - from the Lord out of the heavens. Thus, he overthrew those cities and the entire plain, including all those living in the cities - and also the vegetation in the land. Genesis ch.19 v24-25

The Lord God has control over the raging fire that burns down the cities. Certain scholars have suggested that is from a violent earthquake spewing up asphalt such as it is found in this region of Palestine. The verses suggest that this was coming down from heaven, not from the land because the Lord had decided that the outcry is so great, that their sin is so grievous, so he sent his two angels (see Genesis ch.18 v20-21).

The two angels looked just like men. Angels can look in these cites and reporting back to God for the evil that was going on. God knew and he could see into everybody minds. When the outcry reaches God himself but he waited until he rescued Lot and his family.

He remembered Abraham but only 4 people from two places and they were wiped out from God, the vegetation all around the cities. The fire from heaven must have been tremendous.

- - - - - - -

There the angel of the Lord appeared to him in flames of fire from within a bush. Moses saw that the bush was on fire it did not burn up. So Moses thought, "I will go over to see this strange sight - why the bush does not burn up." Exodus ch.3 v2-3

Moses was an outlaw, he escaped from Egypt because he had rescued a Hebrew from an Egyptian. He was beating the Israelite and Moses had hidden him in the sand. But Pharaoh found out about it (see Exodus ch.2 v11-12, v15).

Moses went to Midian far enough away from Egypt, the Lord was watching him. So God decided to burn a bush but the flames were unusual and the bush stayed alight. Moses went over to have a look. The Lord spoke to him out of the bush, "Moses! Moses!" He knew his name but the earth was indeed holy.

Holiness: involves being consecrated to God and being separated from what you were currently doing.

It burnt with smoke but the source of the fire was unusual it didn't harm the bush.

- - - - - - -

By day the Lord went ahead of them in a pillar of cloud to guide them on their way and by night in a pillar of fire to give them light, so that they could travel by day or night. Exodus ch.13 v21

When the Israelites slaves travelled to the Promised Land by day and night and the Lord kept a watch over them. They could easily slip away and travel by night because the Lord had a pillar of fire which could light them on their way.

Each night if one couldn't sleep, they could look at the fire. God was contemplating and observing them, but he did not sleep. The visible presence of God among his people. The fire would go on until they reached the Promised Land, for well over 40 years.

- - - - - - -

To the Israelites the glory of the Lord looked like a consuming fire on top of the mountain. Exodus ch.24 v17

When they journeyed through the wasteland, they arrived at the Desert of Sinai close to the mountain, where God met with them there. The process of a new nation, Israel and God's instructions of divine law was outlined for Moses who saw and shepherded his people (see Exodus ch.19 v20-21).

The mountain had consuming fire on the top, the fire was the presence of God, but he couldn't be seen. The glory of the Lord was there and the people could marvel at it, but they could not touch the mountain otherwise they would be consumed and die (see Exodus ch.19 v23).

- - - - - - -

Now the people complained about their hardships in the hearing of the Lord, and when he heard them, his anger was aroused. Then fire from the Lord burned among them and consumed some of the outskirts of the camp. Numbers ch.11 v1

After they went from Mount Sinai, they travelled from place to place until the cloud came to rest in the Wilderness of Paran (see Numbers ch.10 v12). The people grumbled about their hardships. But only three days into their march the people made up their complaints about Moses and God.

God was watching them and heard them. For all that God had directed Moses to act and do. They didn't use the roads to go through to the Promised Land because the Egyptian stations and fortresses along the way of the Via Maris. They took the back roads and the path was uneven and scorpions and snakes were there (see Deuteronomy ch.8 v15). Fire from the Lord burned among them from the outskirts of the camp.

God directs the fire against the wicked people (see Psalm ch.21 v9-12). He didn't do it with the Tent of Meeting where many people gathered together. He did it with the outskirts of the camp when they didn't want Moses to hear them.

- - - - - - -

Has any other people heard the voice of God speaking out of fire, as you have, and lived? Deuteronomy ch.4 v33

Nobody has ever seen God. His holiness demands a cloud or covering where he can speak (see Exodus ch.19 v9). Other people think they have found a god, but it turns out not to be there (see 1 Kings ch.18 v26-29). God is majestic and mighty, he created the world and everything in it (see Psalm ch.104). But he didn't see the fearsome God, he doesn't require constant information from man. He only calls when something serious has to be done.

God expects mankind to have a brain and work out what and what the situation is. He has given us the Scriptures with his plan to work to, but man has forgotten to read it. In the Old Testament he has given us the prophets to tell us what should be done, but mankind is not interested in them. The prophets are boring, better to go on holiday and have a good time.

- - - - - - -

For my anger blazes forth like fire and burns to the depths of the grave. It devours the earth and all its crops and ignites the foundations of the mountains. Deuteronomy ch.32 v22 (NLT)

God is holy and his anger rises like fire. Fire is what makes man afraid but when the fire gets going all that man can do is watch. Like the fire on the hills in the summer, or when war breaks out and fire is what they used to set the buildings alight. We have aeroplanes to douse the fire and fire-fighters to control the flames but they are only in specific areas to use, not everywhere all at once.

What makes God so special?

> His anger so is astounding his fire is all around us.
> It burns to the depths of the grave, nobody is safe.
> It devours the earth and everything is wasted.
> It covers all the crops and nothing is left.
> It ignites the foundations and the buildings will collapse.
> It includes the mountains where people go on holiday.

- - - - - - -

God said, "When you have taken the city, set it on fire. Do what the Lord has commanded. See to it, you have my orders." Joshua ch.8 v8

Joshua explains that the Lord directs fire. Don't think that fire is there on the earth God has a hand in it. Eventually the earth and all the people in it will be judged by Jesus and the fire will cover the earth, leave it as a burnt wasteland. Nothing will be safe or secure.

The Lord told the Israelites to wipe out all of the population including the walls and the buildings in the city of Canaan (see Deuteronomy ch.29 v17-18, v25-28). To mark the worship and their evil practices. Nothing will be left. The point is to end the worship of the Canaanite and both men and women must die. The place where they practised it will be a heap of ruins.

- - - - - - -

Then the fire of the Lord fell and burned up the sacrifice, the wood, the stones and the soil, and also licked up the water in the trench. 1 Kings ch.18 v38

Fire can come down from heaven when the prophet Elijah met the Israelites on Mount Carmel. The first bull he offered to the Baal worshippers, but the second bull Elijah repaired the altar of the Lord which was in ruins. Elijah prayed, 'You are indeed God', then the fire came down from heaven and burned up the bull and his sacrifice, even the water which the people had doused on the second bull.

Baal is famous for his storm. Thunder was his voice, lightning was his weapon. But Baal didn't answer, they called on him from morning to noon (see 1 Kings ch.19 v26) but it was no use, he was not a god at all. Elijah made sure that the people would know and understand that. The fire of the Lord consumed everything and they seized all the prophets of Baal and killed them (see 1 Kings ch.18 v40).

- - - - - - -

As they were walking along and talking together, suddenly a chariot of fire and horses of fire appeared and separated the two of them, and Elijah went up to heaven in a whirlwind. 2 Kings ch.2 v11

The chariot and horses of fire they supported the prophet Elijah's ministry and Elisha was allowed to see it. Now at his departure Elijah is taken up by whirlwind to heaven. Like Enoch before him (See Genesis ch.5 v24). There are only two persons in the Bible who experienced departing from the earth while they were still alive.

- - - - - - -

At the time of your appearing, you will make them like a fiery furnace. In his wrath the Lord will swallow them up, and his fire will consume them. You will destroy their inhabitants from the earth, their posterity from mankind. Psalm ch.21 v9-10

King David was the Psalmist and he longs for Israel's complete deliverance from the enemies. Which will come when God deals with the wicked in defence of her victims. It is a prophecy at the end time, the fulfilment of Satan and his band of fallen angels.

King David writes: 'the time of your appearing Lord'. In his wrath the Lord will control them; his free will would consume them. You will destroy them and their inhabitants on the earth. It is a symbol of the time of the end of the age (see 2 Peter ch.3 v9-13).

- - - - - - -

When Solomon finished praying, fire came down from heaven and consumed the burnt offering and the sacrifices, and the glory of the Lord filled the temple. 2 Chronicles ch.7 v1

King Solomon was a good king in his early days and God blessed him with wisdom, such as hadn't been given to all the kings before him. He created the temple of the Lord that was impressive and superb. The ark was brought into the temple (see 2 Chronicles ch.5 v2-13). After that king Solomon was praying by the temple and the people listened to what he said. God sent fire down and consumed all the offerings and the Lord was there in the temple. It burst like lightning and consumed all the sacrifices. Lightning goes up from the earth to heaven, but God sent his flames down on Solomon's temple, it was a marked difference.

- - - - - - -

The Lord Almighty will come with thunder and earthquake and great noise, with windstorm and tempest and flames of a devouring fire. Isaiah ch.29 v6

The prophecy of Isaiah who foretold that in God's time, those nations that devastated Jerusalem will be destroyed. The sudden destruction of the enemy resembled that of the Assyrian army in 701 BC (see Isaiah ch.10 v16).

This example foretold the time of the end. Jesus will finally appear to come back after his death and resurrection. With thunder, earthquake, a great noise like wind, tempest and flames of fire. It was the same vision that king David had (see Psalm 14). Both mentioned the same thought that God will rescue his people from the enemy that overpowered Israel, the time of the battle of Armegeddon (see Revelation ch.19 v11-21).

The promise of God which dates back more than 3000 years still remains and what will happen in the future. Jesus mentioned before his trial and execution, it referred back to the Old Testament, he was reminding the disciples what is going to happen (see John ch.14). It is not new! God foretold this event in king David's time.

- - - - - - -

The sinners in Jerusalem shake with fear. Terror seizes the godless. "Who can live with this devouring fire?" they cry. "Who can survive this all-consuming fire?" Isaiah ch.33 v14 (NLT)

A consuming fire, this is the presence of God regarding judgement for all the people. The prophet Isaiah carries his thinking about the end of time: all 'sinners will shake with fear'. Terror seized the godless, what about the devouring fire? Nothing will be left on earth, it will be wiped clean again. Nothing of man's presence will be left.

God will honour those who he saved by coming to Jesus as Lord of their lives and obeying him (see Romans ch.8 v7-11).

I will gather you and I will blow on you with my fiery wrath, and you will be melted inside her. As silver is melted in a furnace, so you will be melted inside her, and you will know that I am the Lord have poured out my wrath upon you. Ezekiel ch.22 v21-22

You could imagine a furnace, boiling hot because the metal is molten. Thick walls to protect the outside air, steam pouring out of the top. The furnace is to melt the metal. The workers will wear heavy clothing to protect them and the noise is too much to bear.

This is what it will be like for the wicked and the wrath of God. His son Jesus was sinless (see 1 John ch.3 v5) but he died on the cross to save us (see John ch.3 v16-17). Mankind refused to obey Jesus (see John ch.1 v10-11).

I am not surprised that God is very angry and his rage is terrible to behold.

- - - - - - -

Come back to the Lord and live! Otherwise, he will roar through Israel like a fire, devouring you completely. Amos ch.5 v6 (NLT)

God loves us, this is why he left Jesus to come to save us. We have to do it on our own: no parents, no church, no friends to help us. We have to take Jesus as Lord of our lives and obey him whatever the cost. This is the route to take and we would become children of God (see Romans ch.8 v1-17).

There is not much time, our lives on this earth will be very short lived. God is very angry but still patiently waits for the lost.

The axe is already at the root of the trees, and every tree that does not produce good fruit will be cut down and thrown into the fire. Matthew ch.3 v10

Judgement is very near, the axe is carefully sharpened. The first thing God has to do with the axe. Clear the weeds and strike. The tree is widely noticed but the tree does not bear good fruits. What does it mean by 'fruits'?

In the New Testament fruit is like spiritual fruit (see Galatians ch.5 v22-23). The only way you can begin is coming to Jesus for his help with your sorrowful, misery life and he will help you.

It is better for you to enter life with one eye than to have two eyes and be thrown into the fire of hell. Matthew ch.18 v9

The disciples were investigating the greatest in the kingdom of God rather than being like Jesus. He was aware of it and said to them, 'Why don't you be like children?' He called a child and had him stand among them. 'It is better for you not to sin, you don't want to be going into the fire of hell'.

It will be revealed with fire, and the fire will test the quality of each man's work. I Corinthians ch.3 v13

Fire is to decide the quality of each person's work. The fire is God's judgement. The work of some believers will stand the test while the others will disappear. Emphasising the importance of teaching the pure word of God (see the parable of The Talents in Matthew ch.25 v14-30). It will be taken away from you and given to another. You will be thrown outside into the darkness and left without help.

In speaking of the angels, he says. "He makes his angels winds, his servants flames of fire" ... For our God is a consuming fire. Hebrews ch.1 v7, ch.12 v29

Even the angels are flames of fire and like God himself he is a consuming fire. God also exerted his power before the Israelites. He works alongside them to assert victory for the Promised Land and to overthrow the Canaanites (see Deuteronomy ch.9 v3). God cannot be contained, for he himself is a consuming fire burning up the nations that are there sweeping away the wicked who are not willing to obey him.

- - - - - - -

She will be consumed by fire, for mighty is the Lord God who judges her. Revelation ch.18 v8

The fire is a magnificent event, keeping most of the people away. Even the firemen have to be trained in what they do. Most officials and authorised men will protect the people and even let the fire burn itself out if it cannot be contained and shut down. When the wicked die in the lake of fire for ever (see Revelation ch.20 v15).

God will be patient with them but they refused to obey God and repent of their sins (see Revelation ch.16 v9). When God cursed man and woman he said because you haven't obeyed me each individual person will die. They will be cursed by the Lord, he is a God of fire from Genesis to Revelation. There's no surprise when mankind refuses to accept God he would do what he has always done; the flames of fire is a part of man's destruction.

There's a lot of banners and people protesting, marching up and down. God is watching and waiting. He knows that the earth will be destroyed and the wicked will go into the eternal fire. But it is not now. The protesters failed to realise that sin was there all the time, from the beginning to the final end. They don't bother about sin, they ignore it but they should understand the tragedy that mankind has done. God is waiting and soon his eternal fire will be there covering the whole earth.

FOREST

The forest as a large uncultivated tract of land covered with trees and undergrowth.

The battle spread out over the whole countryside, and the forest claimed more lives that day than the sword. 2 Samuel ch.18 v8

Absalom, son of king David was so handsome, there was not a blemish on the boy (see 2 Samuel ch.14 v25). He rose up and he tried to take the kingdom away from king David. The king fled and absconded from Jerusalem and it eventually came to a battle in the forest. Hand-to-hand fighting, but the forest claimed more lives than the sword. The armies apparently became dispersed and many of the men became lost in the forest. Even Absalom on his mule under a wide oak tree got caught by his head (see 2 Samuel ch.18 v9).

He was slain by Joab the commander of the king's army (see 2 Samuel ch.18 v14). Then Joab sounded the trumpet and the battle was finally over, Absalom could never have ascended the throne to remove king David.

- - - - - - -

Then the trees of the forest will sing, they will sing for joy before the Lord, for he comes to judge the earth. 1 Chronicles ch.16 v33

God knows and understands the forest for he created it and made it so. The trees and the undergrowth with bracken and twisted shrubs makes it difficult to see. You can be lost in the forest which way you turn, but there's so many trees all different in nature and purpose. It is a result of the curse of the fall (see Genesis ch.3 v7-18).

King David maintained his praise to the people when he brought the ark of God to his temple in Jerusalem. His covenant, his glory, his temple and his judgement; there the trees of the forest will sing to the Lord his God. Even the trees will sing.

If you have ever been in a forest when the wind blows and the branches and leaves rustle against each other, up and down, flowing thorough the wind it is like a singing to God. It is like a melody and as the wind moves the leaves and branches respond too. Every tree in the forest or land belongs to God.

For every animal of the forest is mine, and the cattle on a thousand hills, I know every bird in the mountain, and the creatures of the field are mine. Psalm ch.50 v10-11

The Lord owns all the animals and birds in the forest and the fields. He watches them when they give birth, he feeds them, he arranges water to flow through the forest and fields (see Job ch.39). When you kill an animal, a bird or fish you are directly responsible to God who made them. You are to care for them and not overrule them (see Genesis ch.1 v26 and Psalm ch.8 v6-8).

If an animal kills a person, you are to stone it to death (see Exodus ch.21 v28) because man is ruler over the animals.

Mankind did not own all the trees, the animals and the birds. God said, 'Rule over it not own it'. We are there with the trees and the animals and birds to look after them.

- - - - - - -

As fire consumes the forest or a flame sets the mountain ablaze, so pursue them with your tempest and terrify them with your storm. Psalm ch.83 v14-15

'God is not silent', said Asaph who wrote the Psalm, 'Why doesn't he finish them off?' It is the reason of God, he knows the hearts and minds of the people. But only the rich and officials wanted Israel to be controlled like their properties, the poor did not want that at all. The Lord sees all the earth, he thinks about the widows, the aliens who would be swept aside. He is silent but he writes it down in his books.

He is mighty and powerful; yes, he can control everything. As fire consumes the forest, he can do that too. What about the hurricane, storms, wind and lightning? Yes, he can do that too. He can do everything he wants, but mankind and the angels he allowed them to choose. Whether they wanted him or not, but God is his wisdom has not interfered with that. We have a choice to make.

- - - - - - -

You bring darkness, it becomes night, and all the beasts of the forest prowl. The lions roar for their prey and seek their food from God. Psalm ch.104 v20-21

When it gets dark in the forest then the wild animals will come and find their food, not by sight but by smell and hearing. Even the owls can find what they need. Silently and swiftly the creatures on the ground will have no real chance to escape. This is not what God wanted, he didn't want the animals preying on each other.

Man's sin got in the way and the world was changed overnight. You will have to take away human sin, it is the only way to make the earth a better place.

- - - - - - -

The remaining trees of his forests will be few that a child could write them down. Isaiah ch.10 v19

So few that even a child on his finger could write them down it is a reference to the Assyrian army that camps and invades a foreign place. It is a terrible thing. War is brutal, trees get in the way so cut them down.

After the two world wars the trees will grow back eventually. It is half a century and you can't stop the trees growing. They will do it all of the time. As the tree nears the winter it stops growing because of the dark and cold. It sheds the final seeds that will grow into trees.

Even if the forest should be destroyed and the city torn down, the Lord will greatly bless his people. Wherever they plant seed, bountiful crops will spring up. Their cattle and donkeys will graze freely. Isaiah ch.32 v19-20 (NLT)

When the Assyrian Empire finished its decline and was finally over this is what the verse means. If the forest is gone the Lord will comfort Israel. Let the seeds be planted again and let the domestic animals, feed. The whole earth will have trees in the end of time and they will come again.

This is what the Sovereign Lord says: The people of Jerusalem are like grapevines growing among the trees of the forest. Since they are useless, I have thrown them on the fire to be burned. Ezekiel ch.15 v6 (NLT)

The prophet Ezekiel was taken away from Jerusalem in 597 BC, he went into exile because the reign of Judah was so poor, basically they were all wicked men. The destruction was harsh, cruel and overlooked none of the important cities of Judah.

He was a prophet and a priest, he warned that Jerusalem would be finished and that God would treat them severely with king Zedekiah (see 2 Chronicles ch.36 v11-14). 'Since they are useless' that is a strong word. It was a forest and they failed to produce good fruit.

- - - - - - -

May I have a letter to Aspah, keeper of the king's forest, so he will give me timber to make beams for the gates of the citadel by the temple and for the city wall and for the residence I will occupy? Nehemiah ch.2 v8

The exile was finally over, Cyrus, king of the Medes took over the Babylon Empire, he published a royal decree in 537 BC. Each king of the Medes had a person overseeing the king's forest. When Nehemiah asked about the city of Jerusalem, he spoke to the king and asked for a letter to give to Aspah who was in charge of the forest. Nobody could cut down the trees that belonged to the king.

The king granted his requests. He was a cupbearer to the king but he asked for a leave of absence. King Artaxerxes was pleased that he remembered the city where he had been taken and gave him army officers and cavalry (see Nehemiah ch.2 v9). He was gone a long time as the king Artaxerxes appointed him governor of Judah (see Nehemiah ch.5 v14). He could cut down the forest as he was the governor.

- - - - - - -

Consider what a great forest is set on fire by a small spark. The tongue is also a fire, a world of evil among the parts of the body. It corrupts the whole person, sets the whole course of his life on fire, and is itself set of fire by hell. James ch.3 v5-6

This is the only verse from the New Testament which refers to a forest. It is the tongue which burns like a fire. It is the evil coming out of the person and it makes no difference whether the person is good or bad. If the tongue is mute or silent most people will approve of the person, but when the tongue speaks, it is like a spark that will burn up a forest. The damage that the speaking voice gives out it will be the voice of hell. It is difficult to stop and retain the tongue. It needs the Holy Spirit (see Romans ch.8 v9)

The sinful mind is hostile to God. It does not submit to God's law, nor can it do so. Those controlled by the sinful nature cannot please God. Romans ch.8 v7-8

Nobody can please God, but the tongue is an evil thing. It comes out of the body and mind of the person. We all are cursed by God and the tongue speaks what we think, but it isn't good.

GRASS

Grass is the area planted with growing, undulating grasses includes a lawn or a meadow.

He fell asleep again and had a second dream: Seven ears of corn, healthy and good, were growing on a single stalk. After them, seven other ears of corn sprouted - thin and scorched by the east wind. The thin ears of corn swallowed up the seven healthy, full ears. Then Pharaoh woke up; he had been a dream. Genesis ch.41 v5-7

Pharaoh dreamed that he was subject to the corn in the field being wiped out. It was a plague that was widespread even covering Egypt and Palestine. It is not new or recent, it happened 4000 years ago. Seven years of the plague then the corn will recover. Seven long, hard years as the corn did not respond to treatment and the Egyptian people begged Pharaoh to help them. They even sacrificed livestock, our bodies and their land.

Joseph reduced the Egyptians to servitude but not the priests (see Genesis ch.47 v21-22). He did that to remind the Egyptians that he had been locked in prison but he was innocent of the charges that Potiphar who was one of Pharaoh officials had made.

- - - - - - -

Let my teaching fall like rain and my words descend like dew, like showers on new grass, like abundant rain on tender plants. Deuteronomy ch.32 v2

The grass needs rain and so does God's teaching. It was the song of Moses because he knew that having a song, kept the Israelites pure and free. God said, 'The people will eventually forsake my words'. The teaching is the first thing that Moses sang. It is important that you teach the words to you family, friends and children.

Can papyrus grow tall when there is no marsh? Can reeds thrive without water? Whilst still growing and uncut, they wither more quickly than grass. Such is the destiny of all who forget God; so perishes the hope of the godless. Job ch.8 v11-13

The destiny of all who forget God. Why is it so important? Why do we have rain and God's presence? (see Revelation ch.9 v20-21)

> The mankind had idols and worshipped demons.
> They think that murder is acceptable.
> They would like to have their magic arts practised.
> Their sexual immorality was common.
> Their thefts, stealing, robbery and fraud.

This is why the reason that men and women are doomed to fail. God would not have them in his kingdom which was pure, righteous and holy.

For like the grass they will wither, the green plants they will soon die away. Psalm ch.37 v2

Like grass they will wither away and die. Nobody cares for the past, it doesn't matter if you were rich and wealthy. The end result is that you will pass away. Did you know the hospitals were the consequences of believers who looked after the poor? Look back and you will find the history, the names of the hospitals will tell you. Certain individuals cared for the people and went out of their way to help them. But now, they were forgotten.

As for man, his days are like grass, he flourishes like a flower of the field; the wind blows over it and it is gone, and its place remembers it no more. Psalm ch.103 v15-16

He flourishes like a 'flower of the field'. God knows and he has written in his books. Jesus said, 'Store up for yourself treasures in heaven' (see Matthew ch.6 v20). It is the plural of the word 'treasures' and it is more than one event and it will keep on going until we die. In the past we looked for God, but what about in the present and the future?

- - - - - - -

They are like plants in the field, like tender green shoots, like grass sprouting on the roof, scorched before it grows up. 2 Kings ch.19 v26

When king Hezekiah ruled over Judah he was a good person (see 2 Kings ch.18 v5-6). But Hezekiah rebelled against the Assyrian empire and did not serve him (see 2 Kings ch.18 v7). Sennacherib, king of Assyria with his army surrounded Jerusalem. Then the prophet Isaiah sent a message to Hezekiah and God heard what Sennacherib had said in blasphemy against him. Sennacherib would not be able to overcome Jerusalem. The angel of the Lord would pass over the camp of the Assyrians and put to death 185,000 men in one night while they were surrounding the city.

The Greek historian Herodotus attributed the destruction to a bubonic plague (see the whole fall in Isaiah ch.37 v21-37). It was it was a very quick work. God had promised king David that he would defend his city (see Isaiah ch.37 v35). God said, 'Have you not heard this, now I have come to do it? The grass in the field will be silenced before it grows up'. Scorched in the sun beating down upon the army.

The grass withers and the flower fall, but the word of God stands for ever. Isaiah ch.40 v8

The plans and purposes of the nations will not prevail. Only God's plans will last it will be a comfort for Israel. Nations will come and go, rulers and authorities will be a freedom from worry, or not. Kingdoms will only last a little while and then they would be gone. Even a mighty republic or society will reign over all the earth, but will be past and gone.

Only God will stand for eternity, for ever. It is the Bible that has the key. If you want to read and study the Scriptures. To show what God can do from Genesis to Revelation it is all there, you will have to take time to study it.

How long will the land lie parched and the grass is every field be withered? Because those who live in it are wicked, the animals and birds have perished. Moreover, the people of are saying, "He will not see what happen to us." Jeremiah ch.12 v4

When the prophet Jeremiah spoke, he knew that the wicked will prosper and the animals and birds will have died. So why did he have a complaint with God? The Lord said to him, 'I will abandon my house and I will uproot them from the land' (see Jeremiah ch.12 v5-17).

Jeremiah understood what God had been saying. That the people of Judah would be taken into exile and would go to Babylon. The empty Promised Land would be there for seventy years. Most of the people will die in Babylon and the children will come back to the land from which they had come. Only a remnant (see Isaiah ch.10 v20-23). Said God, 'It will be a desolate wasteland'.

Then the remnant left in Israel will take their place among the nations. They will be like dew sent by the Lord or like rain falling on the grass, which no one can hold back and no one can restrain. Micah ch.5 v7 (NLT)

The prophet Micah came during the reigns of Kings Jotham, Ahaz and Hezekiah in Judah, as Micah influenced the small towns and villages of his homeland. He said a remnant will appear like the 'rain falling on the grass'.

But the people didn't understand what he meant. He had a prophecy of what the outcome of the nations will bring about. Is about 150 years before it came to pass.

- - - - - - -

The hot sun rises and the grass withers; the little flower droops and falls, and its beauty fades away. In the same way, the rich will fade away with all of their achievements. James ch.1 v11 (NLT)

In the New Testament, little is told about grass. The rich will fall away as the flower droops and the grass is finally dead. This is a sign of what is to come. All the rich think that they control the world but if effect they don't. Satan has a power over mankind but his strength is only limited by God. The achievements of what they have done, in medicine, power and weapons and even Satan, all will come to nothing and be gone.

They were told not to harm the grass of the earth or any plant or tree, but only those people who did not have the seal of God on their foreheads. Revelation ch.9 v4

In the last book when the final chapter is about to begin. God has decided to finish the earth and he has certain plagues to come on the people:

> The seals (see Revelation ch.6 - ch.8).
> The trumpets (see Revelation ch.8 - ch.9).
> The bowls (see Revelation ch.16).

The apostle John saw the demonic locusts coming up out of the abyss (see Joel ch.2 v1-12 and Revelation ch.9 v1-11). God loves the trees, plants and the grass in the fields and the demonic locusts were not told to harm them. They could focus on the wicked who didn't respond to God. Mankind and Satan are not able to remove all the trees, plants and grass, it will be there at the end.

The rest of mankind did not appear to repent of the work of their hands (see Revelation ch.9 v20-21), God decided to end it all and they were all killed (see Revelation ch.19 v21). The earth will not get better, it will get worse before Satan has a chance to get even with God. Satan will lose up to the battle of Armegeddon and the people would be finished. The dead would go to the judgement and then the books will be read.

LAND

The land is a solid portion of the surface of the earth, a country or a nation of people.

God called the dry ground "land" and the waters "seas". And God saw that it was good. Then God said, "Let the land sprout with vegetation—every sort of seed-bearing plant, and trees that grow seed-bearing fruit. These seeds will then produce the kinds of plants and trees from which they came." And that is what happened. The land produced vegetation—all sorts of seed-bearing plants, and trees with seed-bearing fruit. Their seeds produced plants and trees of the same kind. Genesis ch.1 v10-12 (NLT)

In the beginning God created the earth. He decided to let the dry ground be 'land'. In God's plan with shoots of vegetation, plants and trees and that is what happened. The plants and trees produced flowers and berries. The seeds go into the ground and produce varieties of their kind. Not the evolution that man has dreamed up. It is 'plants and trees' that God created with several different kinds; it is plural.

The earth was formed out of water (see 2 Peter ch.3 v5) and founded upon the rivers. The seas are not to cross the boundaries set for them by God like sand (see Psalm ch.104 v9 and Jeremiah ch.5 v22). There is no 'big bang' something made up by men who fail to see what God has created.

But streams came up from the earth and watered the whole surface of the ground. Genesis ch.2 v6

It was very good, but the land had to have water to let the plants and trees grow. So God created the streams flowing up from the earth. But the rain didn't appear first of all, it came later when God created the 'rain' (see Genesis ch.2 v5).

- - - - - - -

Everything that breathed and lived on dry land died. God wiped out every living thing on the earth—people, livestock, small animals that scurry along the ground, and the birds of the sky. All were destroyed. Genesis ch.7 v22-23 (NLT)

When Noah built his ark together with his family and the ark floated above the water for a hundred and fifty days while the earth was in flood (see Genesis ch.7 v24). No plants and trees were there, they were all sodden but they still had life in them, underwater but still they lived. Man, animals and birds died.

The earth was there and the water flowed back into the seas. The animals and birds in the ark could repopulate the earth. God's gift at creation was taken away because of man's sin. Because of the violence that mankind has projected in his worthless and evil life (see Genesis ch.6 v13).

- - - - - - -

God will surely come to your aid and take you up out of this land to the land he promised on oath to Abraham, Isaac and Jacob. Genesis ch.50 v24

Joseph said, 'God will rescue you', as God promised to his forefathers. Joseph, he did not forget what will happen to all Israel. They were in Egypt living by the Goshen territory happily tending their flock of sheep. The grass was good close by the Mediterranean Sea and the rivers flowing through the country.

The Lord will take you out of Egypt to fulfil his promised to Abraham. This is a covenant matter between God and Abraham (see Genesis ch.22 v17-18). Later, they were ill-treated and made to be slaves of the Pharaoh. They didn't remember Joseph and what he had done for the Egyptians to feed them, care for them during the seven years of famine. The plagues in Egypt (see Exodus ch.7 - ch.11) and then the Israelites were free to go back to Palestine. The Pharaoh and the Egyptians drove them out (see Exodus ch.12 v31-33).

- - - - - - -

If you follow my decrees and are careful to obey my commands, I will send you rain in its season, and the ground will yield its crops and the trees of the field their fruit. Your threshing will continue until the grape harvest are the grape harvest will continue until planting, and you will eat all of the food you want and live in safety in your land. Leviticus ch.26 v3-5

There in the Wilderness of Sinai, God met them there and said that, 'In the Promised Land they would have more than enough to eat'. The obedience is the explanation for a blessing from God. There was enough space to plant and reap God's grace was sufficient for all of them.

However, Moses spoke to all the Israelites to promise them God's goodness and his curses (see Deuteronomy ch.28). If they wanted God's blessing to come upon them, they had to obey God and his commandments. If they didn't, they would be wasted away. It is the same today, if men can't worship God and obey his commandments then there will be hunger and thirst and all the people will die. Whereas when the rains don't come for some people, there will be famine. Not necessarily the people affected by them, it is the people who are forgetting God and his blessings.

The tribe of Levi was to carry the sacred objects when they moved away. The other tribes were not allowed to help them. God was holy and righteous so he decided to appoint the tribe of Levi as his helpers. The Levites had a mission for a reward of obedience and a punishment for disobedience, to honour God and follow his commands by tithing.

- - - - - - -

The righteous will inherit the land and dwell in it for ever. Psalm ch.37 v29

When king David wrote this Psalm, the righteous will live in the Promised Land. Their children and their children's children in contrast to the wicked and the evil will not inherit the land. The promises of God contrast the righteous and the wicked:

> Righteous will get God's blessing.
> Wicked will get nothing from God.

There are several wicked people, they are very rich and have significant properties. They run slaves and have plenty to do storing up grain. They think they will inherit the land. But God in his wisdom, he will cast out the wicked as exiles, going away from his Promised Land, ending up broken and destitute in a country of a strange language (see Lamentations ch.1). It might take a long while, but God will do it.

There is no faithfulness, no love, no acknowledgement of God in the land. There is only cursing, lying and murder, stealing and adultery; they break all bounds, and bloodshed follow bloodshed. Because of this the land mourns, and all who live in it will waste away; the beasts of the field and the birds of the air and the fish of the sea are dying. Hosea ch.4 v1-3

There's no acknowledgement of God in the land of Israel. All of the promises have become curses (see Deuteronomy ch.28). Even the animals, birds and fish have lost their lives, they just fade away and be gone. Man is powerful, man is strong but he is no match for God.

The prophet Hosea wrote this book about 720 BC, before the Assyrians and Babylonians came to power and exercised their dominance over the people of Palestine. God's purpose was to let Israel and Judah go into exile because they didn't follow the commands of the Almighty. He was not slow, but he patiently waited until the kings and their subjects, but he sent prophets among them to warn them of what he was about to do.

The Lord was grieved that he had made man on the earth, and his heart was filled with pain. Genesis ch.6 v6

You trample on the poor and force him to give you grain. Therefore, though you have built stone mansions, you will not live in them, though you planted lush vineyards, you will not drink their wine. Amos ch.5 v11

The people don't really matter, it is only getting richer. They 'break all bounds' to acquire property and wealth. The prophet Amos wrote this account because he was worried about the justice and righteousness of this people. He was appalled at what his people were doing.

I am planning disaster against this people, from which you cannot save yourselves. You will no longer walk proudly, for it will be a time of calamity. In that day men will ridicule you; they will taunt you with this mournful song: "We are utterly ruined; my people possession is divided up. He takes it from me! He assigns our fields to traitors." Micah ch.2 v3-4

God assigns our 'fields to traitors' and we are 'utterly ruined'. This is what the people think, but it is very wrong. They failed to protect the prophets of the Lord who came to them, warned about what they were doing (see Jeremiah ch.7 v25-26). In their greed and meanness, they think God doesn't notice, but he was watching them all the time. He knows when they shut the door on the poor and leave them to go away, he looks at the widow and she hasn't anybody to help her.

Lord, you poured out blessings on your land! Psalm ch.85 v1 (NLT)

The Promised Land is truly God's the people are only there for the Lord. The hills and mountains were God reigns, where the Lord will reign forever (see Psalm ch.68 v15-16). The chariots of God are more than most men have; the Lord will fight for his sanctuary and his dwelling is in Jerusalem.

Your silver and gold will not save you on that day of the Lord's anger, For the whole land will be devoured by the fire of his jealousy. He will make a terrifying end of all the people on earth. Zephaniah ch.1 v18 (NLT)

No wealth can save you on that day when God will make a final judgement on the nations and on the peoples of the world. When you die, you don't take anything with you. No gold or silver, nothing. No gold ornaments, no ships or carriages. It is only you that will come up against God. The books were opened and God will look at you and remember what you did on the earth, both secret and hidden (see Hebrews ch.4 v13).

- - - - - - -

The land you are entering to possess is a land polluted by the corruption of its peoples. By their detestable practices they have filled it with their impurity from one end to the other. Ezra ch.9 v11

Do not think that God was wiping out the Canaanites because of their awful practices and evil deeds? If the nations were good, God would leave them alone, but the Canaanite were evil and God's holy people should destroy them utterly (see Deuteronomy ch.7 v1-6). With the idol worshippers of Canaan, their religious ideals they might turn them away from the true God. Like King Solomon did with his wives (see I Kings ch.11 v1-8).

The people living in darkness have seen a great light; on those living in the shadow of death a light has dawned. From that time on Jesus began to preach. "Repent, for the kingdom of heaven is near." Matthew ch.4 v16-17

Jesus said, 'Repent for the kingdom has come'. The people must repent because God's reign was drawing near in the person and ministry of Jesus Christ. What does repentance mean?

Repentance: it is a change of mind and heart thinking about what the Lord has done with his death and rising again. It means being willing not to follow the old way of life, being stopped from doing evil things. It means a turning round from what is wrong, following the path to a new life.

Jesus said: "No good tree bears bad fruit, not does a bad tree bear good fruit. Each tree is recognised by its own fruit." Luke ch.6 v43-44

The 'fruit' is what matter most, whether you go out with your friends, neighbours or even go to work. The 'fruit' that you offer will be good and the Holy Spirit will help you. But you have to turn to Jesus to help you turn the bad fruit into good fruit. Each tree (like you) has to be good or bad.

What would you be saying to God when he comes to judge just you? Are you good or bad?

PANIC

Panic that is a sudden fright or a great terror often without any visible means of a basis or fact.

The Lord will strike you with madness, blindness, and panic. You will grope around in broad daylight like a blind person groping in the darkness, but you will not find your way. You will be oppressed and robbed continually, and no one will come to save you. Deuteronomy ch.28 v28-29 (NLT)

When Moses said to the nation before they entered the Promised Land there are two sorts of people, one who will obey the Lord your God and those who didn't. It is the verses that show what the wicked do:

> They grope about and are blind.
> They are not able to find their way.
> They will be oppressed.
> They will be robbed continuously.
> Nobody can help them.

Panic will strike the wicked. The evil and wicked persons are there in the earth and we can see them. The thought that they may panic and they don't see that God can help them, if they come to Jesus. But sadly, they don't, the panic grips them tightly and they can't see the truth what the Scripture teaches. 'They are not even able to see the way of truth'.

Then panic struck the whole army - those in the camp and field, and those in the outposts and raiding parties - and the ground shook. It was a panic sent by God. 1 Samuel ch.14 v15

God will attack the Philistines, not by men and the 'ground shook' where they were. It was an visible jarring like an earthquake. Other situations by the Lord's influence in nature, the waters, the clouds, the thunder, the whirlwind and the lightning (see Psalm ch.77 v16-18). Don't think that Satan has all the power, he doesn't. But God does, he manifests himself by all the might and strength that comes with what we know today, even the lightning. What power does God have at his control?

God is in control of the creation, he made it so even before man and Satan with his fallen angels came along.

- - - - - - -

But if you turn away from them, they panic. When you take away their breath,

they die and turn again to dust. Psalm ch.104 v29 (NLT)

The Psalm was a hymn to the creator, his theme is the visible world around him that God maintains life on earth. As displayed in his magnificence where God takes away the breath of life and all such beings would die. Animals, birds, fishes and mankind would be ended, be gone to dust. If God is really there, he holds us in his hand and cares for us. When it is finished and it is over, he takes away his breath and man dies. It is the same thought as in the first book of the Bible:

The Lord God formed the man from the dust of the ground and breathed into his nostrils the breath of life, and the man became living being. Genesis ch.2 v7

When a person has died the same body parts are there, but the breath of life is gone and never to be returned. You don't think about that for the animals, but it is the same. The breath of life is to live peaceably on this earth. Live and die, each one has God's breath in it, even a fly or a wasp. We think that is only the big animals that die. He notices even the smallest creature, gives and takes the breath away, like a worm or fly. This is why we need to take care of the animals and birds, big and small. God notices everything.

- - - - - - -

The Assyrians will be destroyed, but not by the swords of men. The sword of God will strike them, and they will panic and flee. Isaiah ch.31 v8 (NLT)

The Assyrian army the mighty military force, soldiers, troops and infantry with one angel from the Lord put to death overnight 185,000 men (see Isaiah ch.37 v36). When the Assyrian army woke up the following morning there was all the dead bodies around. Someone had to bury them but it will take a long while. One angel from God, they will panic and flee back away to their homes right up north.

This was true, one angel from God seized all the mighty army that Assyria had and dealt overnight with one blow. It follows the Egyptian army led by

Pharaoh and it was dealt with by God (see Exodus ch.14 v23-28). It is a fearsome thing to fall into God's hands. Two complete armies struck by fear and panic from God.

"Their flocks and tents will be captured, and their household goods and camels will be taken away. Everywhere shouts of panic will be heard: 'We are terrorised at every turn!' Run for your lives," says the Lord. "Hide yourselves in deep caves, you people of Hazor, for King Nebuchadnezzar of Babylon has plotted against you and is preparing to destroy you." Jeremiah ch.49 v29-30 (NLT)

The King Nebuchadnezzar of Babylon who took away the Assyrian empire that fell with surprising rapidity. The city of Babylon was close to the city of Assyria. King Nebuchadnezzar was due to come down in Israel along to the road near the Mediterranean Sea. There are two places where Hazor is mentioned one in Naphtali and one in Benjamin. It will be probably be the one in Naphtali, that is up north. Panic for the Babylonians are coming.

- - - - - - -

Then all the people of Judah, from the least to the greatest, as well as the army commanders, fled in panic to Egypt, for they were afraid of what the Babylonians would do to them. 2 Kings ch.25 v26 (NLT)

Gedaliah was brutally murdered. The people of Judah fled to Egypt because they were afraid of what the Babylonians will do to them. Egypt was not far way from King Nebuchadnezzar of Babylon. After Palestine, Egypt was the next state to be overthrown (see Jeremiah ch.43 v8-13).

The least to the greatest even the army commanders because they killed Gedaliah whom Nebuchadnezzar had left behind in Israel (see 2 Kings ch.25 v22). Gedaliah said the people, 'Don't be afraid of the Babylonians, settle down in the land and it will go well with you'. But after seven months, Ishmael who was of royal blood killed Gedaliah, but the people were anxious and afraid. Panic struck the people of Judah.

- - - - - - -

At that time, I will send swift messengers in ships to terrify the complacent Ethiopians. Great panic will come upon them on that day of Egypt's certain destruction. Watch for it! It is sure to come! Ezekiel ch.30 v9 (NLT)

For that day is near when king Nebuchadnezzar struck Egypt. He will come and bring death, captivity and the sword. He will set fire to the temples of the gods in Egypt. There will be certain destruction: 'it is sure to come'. Even the prophets Jeremiah and Ezekiel foretold what Egypt would be doing. They were focusing on the wrong sort of gods and they had temples to them.

A temple needs to be constructed and it takes a long while. They had more than one temple. The Babylonians will set their temple over the very spot near to Pharaoh's palace where Nebuchadnezzar had his throne. Panic for the Babylonians are coming to Egypt.

- - - - - - -

*"On that day I will strike every horse with panic and its rider with madness."
declares the Lord. "I will keep watchful eye over the house of Judah, but I will
blind all the horses of the nations." Zechariah ch.12 v4*

It is the day of the battle of Armegeddon. Judah will be besieged as well as Jerusalem. The whole earth would be gathered before Jerusalem. But God will be there and strike the horses and nations with blindness, so they can't see. The beast and the false prophet will be taken away and dealt with. Satan will be bound with one angel and cast him into the Abyss for 1,000 years. Not hundreds of angels, but just one. After that, Satan will go out deceiving the nations in his desperate measure to deal with God. He will be finished, ended up going into the burning fire (see Revelation ch.19 v19-21; ch.20 v7-10).

It is all there in the Scriptures, all you have to do is to study and read the Bible.

*On that day men will be stricken by the Lord with great panic. Each man will
seize the hand of another, and they will attack each other. Judah too will fight at
Jerusalem. Zechariah ch.14 v13*

Panic for all the nations will be against Jerusalem, this will be the time when Satan tries to get even with God. But Satan fails even with his mighty army.

- - - - - - -

*"When you hear of wars and insurrections, don't panic. Yes, these things must
take place first, but the end won't follow immediately." Luke ch.21 v9 (NLT)*

Jesus said, 'Because you hear of wars and revolutions' there will be things at the start of the final time. It doesn't matter when you learn about their things but the end will follow immediately. The insurrection is an uprising by the people and a riot will take place. There will be a mutiny and a revolt and many people will be hurt. They want it badly and they will overcome many obstacles, gather in crowds to protest.

It is like what we see today. Many people want what they can get out of it, most authorities didn't see what it could be like. Many are opposed to any form of discipline, they see themselves as doing what God wanted. They are deluding themselves with banners and marches trying to get the other people who want to get on with their lives. It is always a false belief, a misconception a deception. The reason is that they don't study the Scriptures, the voice of God in the Bible.

Jesus said it about 2000 years ago! Panic will be coming to the crowds who wanted to change all of it and get rid of the past.

RIVERS

Rivers that are a large quantity of water flowing over the land, streams are a small body of water.

He will not enjoy the streams, the rivers flowing with honey and cream. What he toiled for he must give back uneaten; he will not enjoy the profit from his trading. Job ch.20 v17-18

Then Zophar his friend, replied to Job, 'He is a proud and healthy prosperous man'. For in his view, that in itself is proof of his goodness and righteousness. The happiness of the wicked will always be brief and elusive. It is a common theme in wisdom literature; but it is not the truth (see Hebrews ch.11 v32-40).

God had planned something better, not in this world but later. A Garden of Eden for the righteous when the judgement is over and the wicked are condemned and sent to hell, where God is not even there.

- - - - - - -

It was you who opened up spring and streams; you dried up the ever-flowing rivers. Psalm ch.74 v15

It was a Psalm of Aspah, leader of one king David's Levitical choirs. They were dominated by the theme of God's rule over his people and the nation of Israel. Why have you rejected us for ever? There he finds words to view God's overruling power (see Psalm ch.74 v1). He says, 'It was the Lord who created all the rivers'. He went back to the very beginning and reminded God as a king from of old. God watched him carefully and thoughtfully and so Asaph wrote this prayer.

I will set his hand over the sea, his right hand over the rivers. Psalm ch.89 v25

The author was no doubt a Levite, one of Judah's sons who voiced this agonising prayer as a spokesman for the nation. It is the same thought as Psalm 74. How long will you hide yourself away for ever? Remember how fleeting is my life, I am only there for a moment (see Psalm 89 v46-47).

God is over all the rivers his right hand is always there. As the rivers flow down to the sea over obstacles and waterfalls, God is there looking at the flowing water. His right hand guides the rivers where they should go.

- - - - - - -

He turned rivers into a desert, flowing springs into thirsty ground, and fruitful land into a salt waste, because of the wickedness of those who lived there. Psalm ch.107 v33-34

We don't know who wrote this Psalm. It is an exhortation to praise the Lord for his unfailing love in that he hears the prayer of those in need and saves them. It was composed for liturgical use at one of Israel's annual religious festivals. What the Psalmist is saying: that God is prepared to turn the rivers into a waste product that will have no use. He doesn't always guide the rivers down to the sea but he always has a use for them.

When the Israelites were moving from Egypt to the Promised Land, they had to go over waste land, deserts and a wilderness. Where there was little sparse trees, spiders and scorpions frequently roamed the land. It was the Wilderness of Paran for about one hundred miles. There was no water for the community and the people gathered to oppose Moses and Aaron (see Numbers ch.20 v2). Moses raised his arm and struck the rock twice with his staff and water gushed out and the community and their livestock drank. (see Numbers ch.20 v11). God knew there was water under the rock.

The rivers come and ago over the years, many rivers dry up and the rivers change their courses to flow into the sea. Water was there but the community really didn't understand. How could they?

- - - - - - -

Rivers run into the sea, but the sea is never full. Then the water returns again to the rivers and flows out again to the sea. Everything is wearisome beyond description. No matter how much we see, we are never satisfied. No matter how much we hear, we are not content. Ecclesiastes ch.1 v7-9 (NLT)

King Solomon realised that if the rivers flow into the sea eventually the sea would fill up and cover the land. He didn't know that the sea gave up moisture for the clouds, that gave rain over the mountains and hills and that produced rivers. He was wise, but he didn't know about the whole earth. He was located in Palestine which had the Mediterranean Sea on its western side.

King Solomon said. 'How much we hear there is more to learn'. He was content to leave God's plan alone. He understood that the rivers belong to God and no man or the devil is able to stop the rivers flowing past. If you block up the rivers, the water spread out over the land and a new path for the rivers to flow down to the sea.

- - - - - - -

I have dug wells in foreign lands and drunk the water there. With the soles of my feet, I have dried up all the streams of Egypt. 2 Kings ch.19 v24 and Isaiah ch.37 v25

King Sennacherib of Assyria surrounded Jerusalem, he made great boasts of what he had done with his army. Desert lands could not have stopped him and the River Nile in Egypt was easily managed. This was a claim to deity. He did it around the walls of Jerusalem and the people heard it. Assyria had been God's tool of judgement against the nations (see Isaiah ch.10 v5-6), but he had risen to be like God himself. Thus, one night an angel went out in the land and destroyed all his army. He went back to his temple of his god in Nineveh and his sons cut him down with the sword (see Isaiah ch.37 v36-38). Mankind cannot stop the rivers flowing down to the sea. Not even king Sennacherib.

- - - - - - -

God will make rivers flow on barren heights and springs within the valleys. I will turn the desert into pools of water, and the parched ground into springs. Isaiah ch.41 v18

God's provision of water (see 2 Kings ch.3 v17-18) is to let the livestock and mankind drink. If we go without food for many days, you will be very hungry (see Matthew ch.4 v2), but if you don't drink you will be dead. Moses had a special arrangement when God spoke to him under Mount Sinai. He was there for 40 days or nights without eating or drinking (see Deuteronomy ch.9 v9).

God gives rivers to let the livestock flourished and even man could drink the water and live.

He (God) rebukes the sea and it dries up, he makes all the rivers run dry ... The mountains quake before him and the hills melt away. The earth trembles at his presence, the world and all who live in it. Nahum ch.1 v4-5

If the mountains quake before the Lord, what about mankind? Man is only a small person on this earth. Do you know how many people are on this earth? God gives his breath to all mankind and he takes it away when they die. God knows the number of people.

The rivers give a clue to what God is his nature and purpose. If the rivers stopped flowing what about man? We need the rivers and woe-betide anyone who is able to stop the rivers flowing. Only God can do that.

- - - - - - -

The third angel poured out his bowl on the rivers and springs of water, and they became blood ... For they have shed the blood of your saints and prophets, and you have given them blood to drink. Revelation ch.16 v4, v6

Why did they become blood? He gave them blood to drink and punishment is fit for the crime (see Isaiah ch.49 v26). During the Babylonian siege of Jerusalem people in the city there was no food (see 2 Kings ch.25 v3). They murdered and persecuted God's prophets (see Acts ch.7 v52) and the believers were slain and killed (see Hebrews ch.11 v33-37).

Blood in the rivers is the result of man's evil ways for corruption and violence. God tried to stop man doing this but the evil ways of man overcame God's commands and the Lord was forgotten.

The sinful mind is hostile to God. It does not submit to God's law, nor can it do so. Those controlled by the sinful nature cannot please God. Romans ch.8 v7-8

It is important that we repeat what the apostle Paul says to the Romans. It carries through what we are thinking. Man is free to do what he thinks is best, but it is always hopeless and wrong. Man doesn't understand what God is doing. He is there is the past and he is there in the future and only man can last about 70 years it is only a small time!

Looking back at the past, we can see nations come and go. What about the Assyrian and Babylonian empires who managed to control all of the known world? Who knows what these two empires are doing? An empire is past and gone. Man has a thought, what about he can control another nation. He arranges planes, tanks and soldiers and many people die as they get caught in the fighting, the bombs drop on their houses and hospitals. Even a man can't match God, he watches what people are doing when they think that they have a plan.

'Those controlled by the sinful nature cannot please God' it would be pointless to try to stop them. The whole thing is a waste of men and many go down and die, but God has his books and the judgement will come.

- - - - - - -

Then I (John) saw a new heaven and a new earth, for the first heaven and the first earth had passed away, and there was no longer any sea. Revelation ch.21 v1

God decides if there is no sea. Only God can control and manage the oceans, not even Satan and his fallen angels could control that. He tried and failed. He only could move the wind over the mountains and stir up the sea to sink Jesus with his disciples (see Matthew ch.8 v23-27). It was a futile gesture. But he didn't have the power over God.

No sea? it separates the nations one from another. Each one has a separate language and keeps the border shut to foreigners. The sea is a dividing principle. In the new kingdom there would not be any sea so there would be one kingdom looking to God as its ruler.

ROCKS

Rocks are that consume a considerable mass of stone.

Then he will ask, 'Where are their gods, the rocks they fled to for refuge?' Deuteronomy ch.32 v37 (NLT)

The Lord's plans for the future are fixed and certain. Sin will be punished in due time and the judgement will come. Satan and his fallen angels might have access to this earth, wreck this place with men's help and cause all that needs to destroy it. The trees, animals and even man is suffering under the weight of the burden, which Satan has engineered to prevent men from God's help and assistance. Satan likes loud protesters, he likes to interfere with God's rulers, he enjoys strikes where mankind suffers.

God says, 'Where are there gods'? Each man tries to find someone he can look to - the job, the house, the cars, the hobbies and all such things. There are no gods and the rocks they fled to, to escape from God.

God said, "I will take vengeance on my adversaries and repay those who hate me." Deuteronomy ch.32 v41

- - - - - - -

But as a mountain erodes and crumbles and as a rock is moved from its place, as water wears away stones and torrents wash away the soil, so you destroy man's hope. Job ch.14 v18-19

Job comments when his three friends gave their opinions on what was the matter with him; how he had forsaken God and had brought trouble on himself. Job maintained that God has 'destroyed his hope'. He asked for God to come to his aid and talk to him. He was indeed suffering with pain from sores from his feet to the top of his head (Job ch.2 v7). He knew that It wasn't God himself, but he didn't understand that it was Satan who tormented him.

Job recognised that even mountains erode water that wears away stones and that God could remove the rocks that hurt him.

- - - - - - -

Man's hand assaults the flinty rock and lays bare the roots of the mountain. He tunnels through the rock; his eyes see all its treasures. Job ch.28 v9-10

Job had his friends try to convince him, by each having twice what they said to him but he answered everything. Job came to the end of his discussions. He said, 'Even if a man tunnels under the mountain passed rocks and come to the treasures in the earth'. Wisdom has been with God who created all of the mountain and knew the value of the wealth and jewels that were there.

He made the mountain, why didn't God help me? I really don't understand what wisdom is and what God thinks. But God through the storm spoke to him and asked him, 'Where were you when I laid the earth?' (see Job ch.38 - ch.42). He asks Job to consider him.

- - - - - - -

When the men of Israel saw that their condition was critical and that their army was hard pressed, they hid in caves and thickets, among the rocks, and in pits and cisterns. 1 Samuel ch.13 v6

It was all due to the Philistines. 3,000 chariots, 6,000 charioteers and soldiers as numerous as the sand of the seashore. Saul remained there and all the troops with him were quaking with fear (see 1 Samuel ch.13 v5, v7). He offered the burnt offering while Samuel was delayed. When prophet Samuel arrived, he said, 'You have not kept the command the Lord your God gave you'. By offering up the Lord's favour by sacrificing the burnt offering (1 Samuel ch.13 v13). Then Samuel left him alone.

King Saul counted the men with him and they numbered about six hundred men (1 Samuel ch.13 v15). But the Lord rescued Israel with Jonathan the son of king Saul. The Lord is mighty and strong and will overcome the multitude. God doesn't need a multitude of men, he can quite easily manage without anyone there. Like illness, famine, wild beasts and so on.

Go into the rocks, hide in the ground from dread of the Lord and the splendour of his majesty. Isaiah ch.2 v10

'In the last days' (Isaiah ch.2 v2). This is a focus on what will happen to the survivors of the earth when God will judge them. They share out his anger and wrath on all his nations. They didn't agree with God and went off on their own. They thought his Bible was picture language, they didn't respond to his prophets, his church was destroyed, his believers were destitute, persecuted and ill-treated (see Hebrews ch.11 v37-38).

'Go into the rocks', hide from God. He has waited a long time for his majesty to be shared and displayed. Everybody will be frightened and scared waiting for the books to be opened when God will judge the nations.

These are the ones who will dwell on high. The rocks of the mountains will be their fortress. Food will be supplied to them, and they will have water in abundance. Isaiah ch.33 v16 (NLT)

It is symbolic of the security found in God (see Psalm ch.18 v1-3). For example: high they would be out of the way of other people, rocks will be their fortress and security, food they don't go out to find meals and water is found in the fortress where they were. These are the ones who God protects, he cares for them who surrounds them and keeps them safe.

- - - - - - -

You people of Moab, flee from your towns and live in the caves. Hide like doves that nest in the clefts of the rocks. Jeremiah ch.48 v28 (NLT)

This was a message about Moab. The effect was bad because she defied the Lord (see Jeremiah ch.48 v42), but good this place will be restored (see Jeremiah ch.48 v47).

Her overwhelming pride and conceit, arrogance and haughtiness this is what makes Moab fail. Hide in the cleft of the rocks, the crevice the fissure where doves go to nest. Flee from your towns, but it is bad, but good.

- - - - - - -

So I will splash her blood on a rock for all to see, an expression of my anger and vengeance against her. Ezekiel ch.24 v8 (NLT)

This was the date the king of Babylon has laid siege to Jerusalem it was the 15 January 558 BC. God had revealed to the prophet Ezekiel the very moment the army of king Nebuchadnezzar had surrounded Jerusalem and God would exercise judgement on king Zedekiah in Judah.

They had splashed blood with what they had been doing and they didn't hide it away. They had Israelite slaves and they were like the 'poor figs'. An account of the wrath of God against the people in Jerusalem (see Jeremiah ch.24).

- - - - - - -

At that moment the curtain of the temple was torn in two from top to bottom.
The earth shook and the rocks split. Matthew ch.27 v51

When Jesus was crucified and finally gave up his Spirit to God that moment the curtain if the temple was torn in two from top to bottom. This means that God was prepared to welcome the believers into the kingdom of God. Because of what Jesus had done on the cross by sacrificing himself for all of us (see Hebrews ch.9 v26).

Eleazar, the son of Aaron was responsible for the priests to make sure that all its holy furnishing and all its holy articles were covered. When the Kohathites, sons of Levi came to move the Tent of Meeting they must not touch the holy things or they will die (see Numbers ch.4 v15-16). It was a strict procedure to guard the holy things from the Israelites.

When the temple is finished by king Solomon entering the Portico underneath the pillars. We moved to the Holy Place with the tables for bread, lampstand and the altar of incense. Then we went to the Most Holy Place guarded by a curtain to protect the ark of the covenant. This was the 'curtain' that was torn down by God, from top to bottom. The earth was moved and shaken and the rocks split open indicating that God would take the believers who trusted in Jesus as Lord and Saviour.

- - - - - - -

Fearing that we would be dashed against the rocks, they dropped four anchors
from the stern and prayed for daylight. Acts ch.27 v29

The apostle Paul's journey to Rome in AD 59-60. They sailed out to sea and were caught in the wind of hurricane force. They could not head into the wind but were driven along by it (see Acts ch.27 v14-15). It lasted a long time, several days in the Adriatic Sea, but the sailors sensed they were heading for land (see Acts ch.27 v27).

In the days of Paul, the ship was wooden, the rocks in the darkness were beneath the ship. So if they were heading for land in the dark, you have to wait for it when it is light to see the rocks underneath. The ship had a steering bar on either side of the stern and they waited for daylight. All the cargo was thrown overboard to lighten the ship, they passed ropes around the ship to hold it together. It was a real risk that they would not make the journey (see Acts ch.27 v17-18).

Last night an angel of the Lord stood beside Paul. God has graciously given you the lives of all who sail with you (see Acts ch.27 v23-24). God was there with his servant Paul with all the work done by the sailors who tried to keep the ship afloat. God understood that everybody was afraid and petrified with fear of what will happen. It was a dangerous thing to go out in a boat to sea after the Fast (see Acts ch.27 v9).

- - - - - - -

Then the kings of the earth, the princes, the generals, the rich, the mighty, and every slave and every free man hid in caves and among the rocks of the mountain. They called to the mountains and the rocks, "Fall on us and hide us from the face of him who sits on the throne and from the wrath of the Lamb! For the great day of their wrath has come, and who can stand?" Revelation ch.6 v15-17

All the rocks would be there at the final end time. The place where God would manifest his presence, even the mighty were departing and going to the mountains and rocks. They didn't have homes to go to, they didn't have any parties and holidays, they were alone and scared, for the wrath and anger of God.

Why did they hide? (see Revelation ch.9 v20-21):
    They did not repent of the work of their hands.
    They carried on worshipping demons.
    They persisted in idols.
    They didn't repent of their murders.
    They pursued magic arts.
    They were involved in sexual immorality.
    They were practised thieves.

They didn't believe God wonders, they ended their days in futility and hopelessness (see Psalm ch.78 v32-33). I am not surprised that they went into the rocks of the mountains. They overlook God and his wondrous creation that we can see. The trees all so different, the animals their colouring and moods, the stars they shine so brightly and so far away. How can they not see?

TREES

Trees are a large plant with a single wooded trunk.

The land produce vegetation: plants bearing seed according to their kinds and trees bearing fruit with seed in it according to their kinds. And God saw that it was good. Genesis ch.1 v12

In the beginning God created the trees before he created man. God loves trees he is certain that the tree will be there for all time. Eventually the trees will reappear when God had judged the world and the earth will be devastated by fire. God selected the kind of trees. Do you know how many trees are in Britain? There are more trees that we can expect to find. There are more than fifty fir trees and pine trees in the northern hemisphere, each one is different from the others. God selected each one as precious to him. This is why he said, 'It was good'. Goodness is a superb, clever and talented work of God.

The Lord God made all kinds of trees grow out of the ground - trees that were pleasing to the eye and good for food. Genesis ch.2 v9

The Lord God didn't choose trees for show, but he selected trees that would bear seeds and fruits that mankind and the animals would enjoy. He created a wide range of trees that each one would have fruits across whether it was hot or cold, warm or flooded, each one had a fruit over the seasons. Trees are not just brown bark and green leaves, they are more than that. Just go out looking for the trees, and 'brown bark' covers all the greys, greens and whites.

But mankind sinned and God had to change all of his creation. It was death all around, even the trees had to fall down and cease growing. Canker, fungus or scale attacked all the trees and like man eventually had to die. This ruined the earth and we have protesters looking around at what we have done and not being very happy about it. It would be there back in the beginning and not just now. Sin causes everybody to die.

- - - - - - -

Throughout Egypt hail struck everything in the fields - both men and animals; it beat down everything growing in the fields and stripped every tree. The only place is did not hail was the land of Goshen, where the Israelites were. Exodus ch.9 v25-26

While Israel was locked away in Egypt and the Israelites groaned in their slavery. God looked at his people and was concerned about them (see Exodus ch.2 v23-25), he decided to do something about Egypt. For example, he had a lot of plagues:

The plague of blood.
The plague of frogs.
The plague of gnats.
The plague of flies.
The plague of livestock.
The plague of boils.
The plague of hail.
The plague of locusts.
The plague of darkness.
The plague on the firstborn.

In the beginning the Egyptians did the things that Moses promised but later the magicians couldn't (see Exodus ch.8 v18). It was only a short time while the plague lasted but Pharaoh hardened his heart and would not let the Israelites go.

This was the worst hail Egypt had ever experienced since it had become a nation (see Exodus ch.9 v24). The flax and barley were destroyed but the wheat and spelt came later and ripened without the Egyptians facing a famine. The hail stripped all of the trees but not In Goshen where the Israelites were. They were sheep farmers and all the sheep were in the field. They were slaves under the Egyptians and would not have collecting the sheep inside, because they were still working.

- - - - - - -

When you enter the land and plant fruit trees, leave the fruit unharvested for the first three years and consider it forbidden. Do not eat it. In the fourth year the entire crop must be consecrated to the Lord as a celebration of praise. Finally, in the fifth year you may eat the fruit. Leviticus ch.19 v23-25 (NLT)

During the long journey when the Israelites came to the Promised Land. God said. 'When you plant a fruit tree you may only harvested it after five years'. The tree has to grow, if you take the fruit, it will be damaged by over-cropping. Pruning the tree leads to a better quality of fruit, shield it from the cold wind and to remove any suckers. The tree has to learn how to gather the fruits.

How is the soil? Is it fertile or poor? Are there any trees on it or not? Do you best to bring back some of the fruit of the land. Numbers ch.13 20

They came to the Promised Land the people expected to go in and the Lord will remove any of the Canaanite inhabitants. They had to go in and explore the land first. When they came back, they said, 'The land is good but the people are fierce and the cities are fortified' (see Numbers ch.14 v26-33). That night all the people of the community wept and grumbled. 'We must go back to Egypt' (see Numbers ch.14 v1-4).

The Lord God said, 'How much longer will this community grumble against me?' Numbers ch.14 v27

God said, 'Your bodies will die before you go into the land'. (see Numbers ch.14 v32-35). It will take forty years while you go into the desert in the Wilderness of Paran. The Lord said, 'You will die in the desert and your children will go into the Promised Land because you didn't trust me'.

- - - - - - -

When you are attacking a town and the war drags on, you must not cut down the trees with your axes. You may eat the fruit, but do not cut down the trees. Are the trees your enemies, that you should attack them? You may only cut down trees that you know are not valuable for food. Use them to make the equipment you need to attack the enemy town until it falls. Deuteronomy ch.20 v19-20 (NLT)

God said, 'Only use the wood to attack your enemies, the spare fruit trees that you can save for yourselves'. The failure of later armies to follow this wise ruling, reduced and cut down the trees included much of the land of Palestine. Because there was fighting because the kings didn't follow the Lord's practice and the land was barren of trees. Like the cedars of Lebanon.

Swarms of locusts will take over all your trees and the crops of your land. Deuteronomy ch.28 v42

It started with Israel's failure to lay completely empty the Promised Land as God had directed (see Judges ch.1 v1-36). God's rebuke for their disloyalty (see Judges ch.2 v1-5). They only stopped pursuing the Canaanites to let them remain in the land, where they worshipped the false idols and let the Israelites do the same. This unfaithfulness led to the exiles. God's promise was that the Israelites should humbled themselves and obey his commands. Locusts will swarm over your land (see Deuteronomy ch.28 v38-42).

- - - - - - -

The trees of the Lord are well watered; the cedars of Lebanon that he planted. There the birds make their nests; the stork has a home in the pine trees. Psalm ch.104 v16-17

In the Promised Land the freely watered Lebanon, with its great trees the birds can nest and the animals can roam freely. The very idea of God's wonderful place. The seasons of life on earth governed by the sun and moon.

The Psalmist theme is the visible creation around him which he sees as God is good with which the invisible creator has clothed himself with wonder and glory. It is a peaceful place where nothing can be trodden down and no waste of other man-made thing can be there.

- - - - - - -

You will cut down every good tree, stop up al the springs, and ruin every good field with stones. 2 Kings ch.3 v19

Israel is going to stop both the wool from Moab and every good tree. This was a heavy annual tribute from Moab. The victor had decided to ruin the country over which he had control and that is not very nice. The war with Moab is going on, but Moab rebelled against Israel thinking that the Ahaziah had died, but he did not have a son to reign after him and that was indeed difficult for Israel (see 2 Kings ch.1 v17).

I will plant trees in the barren desert—cedar, acacia, myrtle, olive, cypress, fir, and pine. I am doing this so all who see this miracle will understand what it means—that it is the Lord who has done this, the Holy One of Israel who created it. Isaiah ch.41 v19-20 (NLT)

God did plant trees for us to enjoy, both amazing and wonder to see and the fruit of the tree with bounty for us to collect. In the barren desert where no-one goes frequently. Every place where God has planted trees, we can see what he has done both in the hot and the cool places. The tree takes about ten to fifteen years to grow to maturity and some of the trees go back a long way in the past.

We rejoice over the trees that God has given to us and they symbolise his goodness to us. His patience, long lasting self-control and tolerance of what we have done with the earth. We have ruined it with the waste, plastics and horrible buildings and the smog over the cities. Still the trees maintain their stature and significance.

- - - - - - -

Many times, I struck your gardens and vineyards, I struck them with blight and mildew. Locusts devoured your fig and olive trees, yet you have not returned to me, declares the Lord. Amos ch.4 v9

The Israelites were hampered with their gardens and vineyards. God did everything he could, he left the trees alone but they were covered by locusts and mildew and the fruit could not be eaten. When you went out to sow, God struck them with blight and the locusts ravaged the land so when you harvested, nothing was there. They continued to sow and harvest but many times God went through the Promised Land and wasted it.

Why? Because the Israelites have not returned to me. If they had, God would bless them and they would have a bumper harvest and the fruit of the trees will be blessed and the locusts would not be there.

I will increase the fruit of the trees and the crops of the field, so that you will no longer suffer disgrace among the nations because of famine. Then you will remember your evil ways and wicked deeds, and you will loathe yourselves for your sins and detestable practices. Ezekiel ch.36 v30-31

God punished the Israel and Judah to go into exile away from their Promised Land. Most people didn't live that long and they died while they were in exile. Some of Judah's children would go back to the Promised Land. The remainder were excited and confident and there was a long journey home to go home back to their land. God said, 'I will increase the fruit of the trees and the crop of the field'. They have to do it all over again, the ground wasted away and the weeds and thorns grew in their fields.

Remember the point of this exercise: 'You will loathe yourselves for your sins'. I will take away the famine that you are prone to when you come to see the damage it takes. It will take a long time for you to recall your sins and detestable practices getting them back to what the state they were in. God doesn't hide your sin for you, you will remember it and look back with disbelief and sorrow.

- - - - - - -

To you, O Lord, I call, for fire has devoured the open pastures, and flames have burned up all the trees of the field. Joel ch.1 v19

The prophet Joel recalled the devastation in the form of a vast plague of locusts and severe drought coming on Judah. He calls on everyone to repent:

"Even now," declares the Lord, "return to me with all your heart, with fasting and weeping and mourning." Joel ch.2 v12

It is the last days, if they do not repent, the fire will sweep across the land and all the fields will be burned up (see Revelation ch.8 v7). It is the wrath and anger of God because the whole world was caught up with Satan and his fallen angels (see Romans ch.1 v18-19). It is important that you repent of your deeds otherwise the Lord will decide that you don't care for the trouble you have caused.

Repent: means turning round from what you have been doing and going to serve God's way. It may cause you to weep and mourn that you failed to see what God's had intended for you to do.

The axe is already at the root of the trees, and every tree that does not produce good fruit will be cut down and thrown into the fire. Matthew ch.3 v10 and Luke ch.3 v9

It involves producing good fruit from the Holy Spirit which he directs for you to do.

- - - - - - -

They are like shameless shepherds who care only for themselves. They are like clouds blowing over the land without giving any rain. They are like trees in autumn that are doubly dead, for they bear no fruit and have been pulled up by the roots. They are like wild waves of the sea, churning up the foam of their shameful deeds. They are like wandering stars, doomed forever to blackest darkness. Jude ch.1 v12-13 (NLT)

This is what the Bible teaches about the false teachers and false prophets. It is a sobering thought. They would be gone like wandering stars, never to achieve what God had wanted; they will be reserved for the blackest darkness. The darkness will be all around you, and nobody will ever call your name. You will be separated from God and his people for ever. They are like trees, like roots pulled up out of the ground and they will be dead. Roots will hold soil but not be able to make a tree, the tree will still be there but it will not have leaves, flowers or fruits.

WOODS

Woods that are a collection of densely growing trees.

Then Jonathan, Saul's son, arose and went to David in the woods and strengthened his hand in God. And he said to him, "Do not fear, for the hand of Saul my father shall not find you. You shall be king over Israel, and I shall be next to you. Even my father Saul knows that." So the two of them made a covenant before the Lord. And David stayed in the woods, and Jonathan went to his own house. 1 Samuel ch.23 v16-18 (NKJV)

If you have one of two trees in a copse or thicket you can see the enemy, you can look through the trees. But not so in a wood. There is a lot of densely growing trees, it covers a wide range of terrain. So Jonathan went to the woods where David was hiding, because Saul, King of Israel had come after him to kill him (see 1 Samuel ch.19 v2). The woods will hide hide David from king Saul. He didn't find David at all but, he searched for him and arranged people to find out where David was (see I Samuel ch.22 v9 and ch.23 v7). Jonathan knew that David had been appointed by the prophet Samuel (see 1 Samuel ch.16 v13) to be king over Israel.

- - - - - - -

For the battle there was scattered over the face of the whole countryside, and the woods devoured more people that day than the sword devoured. 2 Samuel ch.18 v8 (NKJV)

Absalom was trying to get the throne away from king David and there was more fighting. The woods took many more soldiers than the sword and the armies became lost in the woods or the forest. Absalom was overcome in the trees but died and the rest of the battle was over. The Israelites fled to their homes and they threw Absalom into a big pit in the forest and piled up a large amount of stones over him (see 2 Samuel ch.18 v16-17).

- - - - - - -

Then the trees of the woods shall rejoice before the Lord. For He is coming to judge the earth. Oh, give thanks to the Lord, for He is good! For His mercy endures forever. 1 Chronicles ch.16 v33-34 (NKJV)

On earth, several people get away with a lot of evil, or die before the judges can catch up with them. They might be called slave traders, people in authority who are over-ruling the workers, whether they might be slaves or not. They would treat others as if they didn't exist; people have lost their jobs and suffer greatly with no income or future. But the woods know, they are stable in the ground, they are not likely to move and they sing to God when the wind blows.

Finally, God will call them to account in the judgement. People have hidden what should be brought out in to the open; there's many secrets which haven't been told. God knows all that we have been doing, and he writes it down in his books. Each person was judged according to what he had done on the earth and only on the earth and not in Hades or Sheol. There was a book of life and those people who were named in it, were free to go with Jesus, they were spared for the judgement because God had selected them for his children and they were forgiven for all their sins (see Romans ch.8 v37-39; Galatians ch.3 v26).

Jesus said, "All who are victorious will be clothed in white. I will never erase their names from the Book of Life, but I will announce before my Father and his angels that they are mine." Revelation ch.3 v5 (NLT)

All the trees of the woods shall rejoice, because God has pronounced judgement on all men, dead or alive. After death we await the judgement that will come. The trees know that mankind in his sin has a lot to answer for, chopping down the trees to get precious wood, burning wood to make fields, even the trees are mindful of the state of man. They are there to protect more and more animals, birds and animals that live in the woods.

- - - - - - -

As the fire burns the woods. And as the flame sets the mountains on fire. So pursue them with Your tempest, and frighten them with Your storm. Fill their faces with shame. That they may seek Your name, O Lord. Psalm ch.83 v14-16 (NKJV)

God doesn't want anybody to go to hell. This is reserved for Satan, his beast, false prophet and his fallen angels.   But if man persists in his woeful state, ignoring God, seeking idols, hell will await for him.

Jesus said, "For wide is the gate and broad is the road that lands to destruction, and many enter thorough it.   But small is the gate and narrow the road that leads to life, and only a few find it." Matthew ch.7 v13-14

Only a few find the path, the road that leads to life. Most go on the broad road and wide is the gate that leads to hell.   Satan loves it and he rejoices when people die.   But small is the gate and only a few find the narrow path that comes to Jesus as Saviour and Lord of their lives. The woods hide it but most people look for the easy option, they seek pleasure on this earth not seeking God.

For if God did not spare angels when they sinned, but sent them to hell. 2 Peter ch.2 v4

There is no evidence in the Bible that an angel could be saved once he had left his rightful place or assignments. This is the choice that the angels have made, it is a choice to honour God or be free to roam with Satan on earth. There is no going back, no return.   Angels have a choice and several have made a bad choice in following Satan where he goes. Satan makes himself as beautiful and handsome who leads his fallen angels well, but Satan himself is doomed and the Scriptures make it very clear.

- - - - - - -

Let the field be joyful, and all that is in it. Then all the trees of the woods will rejoice before the Lord. For He is coming, for He is coming to judge the earth. He shall judge the world with righteousness. And the peoples with His truth. Psalm ch.96 v12-13 (NKJV)

All the trees of the woods will rejoice. Jesus Christ will come again and he is coming to judge the world. Don't think the trees are mute and speechless, they can rejoice. They would welcome the change that God has in mind; to be free from death and live forever. The branches will rejoice and the leaves will look beautiful.   It is magnificent where a tree has been growing apart and shapes the countryside where his striking and imposing presence.

I will make a covenant of peace with my people and drive away the dangerous animals from the land. Then they will be able to camp safely in the wildest places and sleep in the woods without fear. Ezekiel ch.34 v25 (NLT)

God would make a 'covenant of peace'. For all of God's covenants will be aimed at peace. What is peace?

Peace: is more than absence of hostility, it is fullness that one can enjoy life when protected from security.

The wild animals will wait in the woods will come without warning, frighten people away from their homes. The woods wave around in the wind it gets very dark in the night-time and the noises in the forests get closer to us. This is what fear means and it is frightening because you can't see what is there. The mind is fearful, who knows what will happen? Going out into the woods without expecting dangerous animals, snakes and scorpions to come out looking for you.

In the future, you can rest under the woods and make your home there.

WORLD

The world as in all its inhabitants in this present state of existence.

God observed all this corruption in the world, for everyone on earth was corrupt. So God said to Noah, "I have decided to destroy all living creatures, for they have filled the earth with violence. Yes, I will wipe them all out along with the earth!" Genesis ch.6 v12-13 (NLT)

Everybody was corrupt. So what does corrupt mean?

Corrupt: it means unscrupulous, fraudulent and dishonest. It also includes depraved, crooked and evil.

We were like that. Nothing good can come out from us. We were deceitful and wicked. From the start of life, we get more and more sinful and violent. Each day comes around, we might get even worse. This is what original sin means. We start sinning from the moment we are conceived (see Psalm ch.51 v5). God looked at all the creatures he made. This is why God had enough and wiped the world clean again. But spared Noah who found favour in the eyes of the Lord and his family in the ark, 8 people in the ark (see Genesis ch.7 v13) and tens of thousands didn't make it. The world was badly corrupt.

God said, "Come, let us go down and confuse their language so they will not understand each other." So the Lord scattered them there over all the earth, and they stopped building the city. Genesis ch.11 v7-8

God gave Noah and his three sons, Shem, Ham and Japheth after the flood to populate the earth (see Genesis ch.9 v7). So they constructed the Tower of Babel, to see if they can reach up to God (see Genesis ch.11 v4), but not going out to find areas where they could settle. So the Lord gave each one a different language so they stopped constructing the building. It would be impossible to carry on where as each man couldn't understand what the other people meant. The Lord scattered them over the face of the world, each with his own language and that is what it is today.

- - - - - - -

Then all the nations of the world will see that you are a people claimed by the Lord, and they will stand in awe of you. Deuteronomy ch.28 v10 (NLT)

When the Israelites went into the Promised Land. The River Jordan is the first thing that they might have to cross over. The river flows into the Dead Sea was in flood during the harvest, for the spring rains and the melting of snow on Mount Hermon (see Joshua ch.3 v15).

God said, 'You are a people that I have selected, not because you are mighty or strong but because I have made a covenant with you' (see Deuteronomy ch.26 v16-19). God chose Israel and that choice was unchangeable and fixed for this world. God's purpose will be fulfilled in Israel, but she will have to come to accept the Jesus Christ as her Saviour and Lord (see Romans ch.11 v25-27).

- - - - - - -

For all the earth is the Lord's, and he has set the world in order. 1 Samuel ch.2 v8 (NLT)

God had decided to fix the earth in space going round the sun, even Satan for all his power couldn't move it. The earth is the Lord's and he has set the seasons in order. This is why we know the time when the sun rises and sets, the rotation around the sun to have cold and hot weather as the earth is tilted (see Genesis ch.8 v22).

It was due to God's purpose that we should live on this earth rather than all the planets and stars around us. We are stewards to work and live on this world and not to destroy it by man's excessive greed and damage.

- - - - - - -

King David said, "Give thanks to the Lord and proclaim his greatness. Let the whole world know what he has done ... Let all the earth tremble before him. The world stands firm and cannot be shaken." 1 Chronicles ch.16 v8, v30 (NLT)

God is insistent and the world stands firm and cannot be shaken. The earth will tremble before God but the world stands firm and fixed and 'cannot be shaken'. In king David's time, everybody knows what God has created that we must come before him and tremble. Nobody could say they didn't know, or understand, or the language is unknown. They believe in a God and he is mighty and strong.

The world cannot be shaken out of its existence and it stands firm. Nothing that each man has made can move the earth out of its period to go round the sun. It stands there a solid ball of magnum or rock, it will be embedded and is unshakeable. We could re-engineer it would not make any difference at all to the route of the earth. Summer and winter, day and night the earth might carry on rotating at twenty-four hours a day.

- - - - - - -

There is no speech or language where their voice is not heard. Their voice goes out into all the earth, their words to the ends of the world. Psalm ch.19 3-4

King David has a Psalm of reverence to God. 'The heavens declare the glory of God' (see Psalm ch.19 v1). It is not 'heaven' but heavens, it is plural. The silent heavens speak, declaring the glory of God in his magnificence. The stars tell us what God had done, how far away they are, how big they must have been and the planets going round them. Even now man is struggling to get rockets to the moon. Go out in to the night and you can see the stars stand out in the sky. Hundreds and thousand of stars! God knows what each one is called (see Psalm ch.147 v4).

God sets all the stars in place, like the work of his fingers (see Psalm ch.8 v3). His shining and glorious stars (see Psalm ch.148 v3). The stars don't tell us what God has done, but they each tell us what God is like. Their voice goes out every day when the sun goes down and sets. This is the purpose and nature of God.

- - - - - - -

For when he spoke, the world began! It appeared at his command. The Lord frustrates the plans of the nations and thwarts all their schemes. But the Lord's plans stand firm forever; his intentions can never be shaken. Psalm ch.33 v9-11 (NLT)

God spoke and the world began. The Lord is the creator who by his power imposed his order of his creation, no power or combination of powers can thwart his plan to save his people. God spoils all man's wayward plans and contrary designs. The Lord's plan stands firm, every man can do nothing about it. The judgement is his and he will carry it through. Nobody could argue that it wasn't fair, each one will be presented with what God's books contain and there is nothing hidden that will not come out (see Ecclesiastes ch.12 v14).

He sets the earth on its foundations; it can never be moved. Psalm ch.104 v5

The earth is going to last and be there while we were here, it can never be moved, it will never decay and it will not give way. The foundations are fundamental, if the foundations fail the building will collapse. God says the foundations are secure, nobody or the angels could move or even edge out the earth, the earth is fixed and sure and will rotate about the sun.

The world has been set on God's foundations. Do you know what that means? God has established the earth and it is totally fixed in place. Don't worry a comet or a planet might come close to the earth, but never touch it.

- - - - - - -

That the Most High is sovereign over the kingdoms of men and gives them to anyone he wishes. Daniel ch.4 v32

Most people had a vote for what sort of person they can pick to have authority over them. God selects the person who he believes could make the right sort of plan. God is not like men, men go of and stand in a way, that is not best for them nor us as believers. Men get obstinate and the books of the Bible betray the worst kind of authority over us. Like king Nebuchadnezzar (see Daniel ch.4 v28-37). God knows everything, he selects the best one to carry it through, even though he is limited to the people he can choose or select.

When Jesus was arrested, forced to go to Pilate, he was sentenced and crucified outside of the city. God understood that he must die. Jesus knew and went through his painful death to set mankind free. Nobody knew about it and it was shocking to see him hanging there. Later, they would realise that he suffered there and many people will witness his act of kindness and love.

That is what made the difference in the world and lasted over 2000 years.

- - - - - - -

For what good will it be for a man if he gains the whole world, yet forfeits his soul? Matthew ch.16 v26

Jesus indicated that the soul was the most important thing. Whether we go to heaven or hell. If a man has everything he wanted, but loses his soul to hell, it really matters.

Jesus knew that his final work will be done (see John ch.17 v5), he completed his duty to try to convince men about his Father, but his earthly work was over (see John ch.1 v10-11). There was only about a handful of disciples left in a room where they were staying (see Acts ch.1 v13-14). For three years Jesus taught the people in the countryside, he did certain miracles and he healed the ones who were sick. He knew and understood that his disciples would go into the world to make a difference.

A bright pupil might say that his time was wasted and he didn't have many disciples, but he was wrong. The Holy Spirit came and all through the world he convinced people on earth to follow Jesus, he was only one man based in the Promised Land but he died on a cross to save us. This is what really matters. It is the soul of man that is important.

- - - - - - -

If the world hates you, keep in mind that it hated me first. If you belonged to the world, it would love you as its own. As it is, you do not belong to the world, but I have chosen you out of the world. That is why the world hates you. John ch.15 v18-19

If the world hated Jesus who didn't carry on with what they were doing but he presented the right way to live; most people ignored him. They like his stories and failed to act what Jesus had said (see John ch.6 v60). The Pharisees work to control the religion of the state and they didn't like what Jesus taught. They dismissed him and tried to stop him working (see Acts ch.7 v51-53).

If you come to Jesus as your Lord and Saviour you will have the take the punishment of the world against you, you will be hated for what you believe, like Jesus who was the Son of God.

- - - - - - -

When the Holy Spirit comes, he will convict the world of guilt in regard to sin and righteousness and judgement. John ch.16 v8

The Holy Spirit will help you (see Romans ch.8 v9) and will guide you to what is right for you. The Holy Spirit will convict the world of what they were doing is wrong and being led into sin.

Sin: people can never see themselves as sinners, they have a problem with a failure to believe in Jesus. They don't accept sin as being bad.

Righteousness: this is brought about by Jesus Christ sacrificial death on the cross. When one dies to save another person, this is righteous.

Judgement: the defeat of Satan which was a form of judgement not simply a victory. God will deal with the evil and bad persons on this world.

This is the work of the Holy Spirit. We present the message and the Holy Spirit works in the minds of the people we speak to. If we don't speak, how can they hear? If we stay only remained in the church, how can they believe?

- - - - - - -

For there will be greater anguish in those days than at any time since God created the world. And it will never be so great again. In fact, unless the Lord shortens that time of calamity, not a single person will survive. But for the sake of his chosen ones he has shortened those days. Mark ch.13 v19-20 (NLT)

During those times there will be much more suffering than any time before. In fact, if the Lord hadn't shortened the time nobody would be alive. This was a coming of the Lord to await the power of the resurrection and to face the judgement. This would be the victory over Satan and will be curbed by his downfall in the lake of fire. Christ will reign with his saints who didn't worship the beast for a thousand years. This is the first resurrection (see Revelation ch.20 v4-5). This is the time when the saints on earth will undergo a real suffering for their faith.

- - - - - - -

And then he told them, "Go into all the world and preach the Good News to everyone. Anyone who believes and is baptised will be saved. But anyone who refuses to believe will be condemned." Mark ch.16 v15-16 (NLT)

Every believer should go out and preach the good news to everyone, not remaining or staying in the church building. Jesus said, 'Go out into all the world'. If as believers we don't do it, nobody can be saved. The work of the Holy Spirit is to convince the world of the dangers to come but we have to announce it. 'Preach the word', said Jesus, 'and tell the people what will happen to the lost'.

Yet when I am among mature believers, I do speak with words of wisdom, but not the kind of wisdom that belongs to this world or to the rulers of this world, who are soon forgotten. No, the wisdom we speak of is the mystery of God—his plan that was previously hidden, even though he made it for our ultimate glory before the world began. But the rulers of this world have not understood it; if they had, they would not have crucified our glorious Lord. 1 Corinthians ch.2 v6-8 (NLT)

This was the mystery of God. His plan for our salvation. The people of this world didn't believe it, they thought it was impossible and only for the Jewish nation (see John ch.1 v10-13).

We have to explain to the lost souls in this world:

> There is a God (see Genesis ch.1 v1).
> God is good (see Genesis ch.1 v31).
> We are sinful (see Psalm ch.51 v3-5).
> God is love (see John ch.3 v16).
> God sent his son (see Hebrews ch.4 v14-15).
> Jesus died for our sins (see Romans ch.5 v6-8).
> There is life after death (see 1 Corinthians ch.15 v35-44).
> The Lord will return again (see John ch.21 v22).
> What we do now matters (see Romans ch.1 v28-32).
> There will be a judgement (see Acts ch.24 v25).
> We can be forgiven (see Ephesians ch.1 v7).
> We need to respond (see Revelation ch.3 v20).
> We will have to change (see James ch.2 v14-18).

- - - - - - -

Do everything without complaining and arguing, so that no one can criticise you. Live clean, innocent lives as children of God, shining like bright lights in a world full of crooked and perverse people. Philippians ch.2 v14-15 (NLT)

We are children of God and the Holy Spirit is in our hearts. Everybody should understand that we are holy to the Lord God and serve him patiently (see Matthew ch.6 v33-34). People will notice a difference between those who work for the devil and those who work with Christ. We are like shining, bright lights in the world. We don't have to talk or say anything we show in our lives the Holy Spirit that moves other people to respond.

For ever since the world was created, people have seen the earth and sky. Through everything God made, they can clearly see his invisible qualities—his eternal power and divine nature. So they have no excuse for not knowing God. Yes, they knew God, but they wouldn't worship him as God or even give him thanks. And they began to think up foolish ideas of what God was like. As a result, their minds became dark and confused. Claiming to be wise, they instead became utter fools. And instead of worshipping the glorious, ever-living God, they worshiped idols made to look like mere people and birds and animals and reptiles. So God abandoned them to do whatever shameful things their hearts desired. As a result, they did vile and degrading things with each other's bodies. They traded the truth about God for a lie. Romans ch.1 v20-25 (NLT)

The Lord remembers the works of the devil as foolishness. They are all simply corrupt, evildoers frustrate the plans of the poor (see Psalm ch.14). God abandoned themselves to their shameful things, they did vile actions against other people. They traded themselves for a lie, but thought they were being wise. It will get worse not better. Worshipping the glorious ever-living God who made us he gave his breath to make us alive, but man abandoned him for whatever shameful things he did with each other. They traded life with God for a life without God and suffered a miserable event. Like what the Israelites did when they entered the Promised Land, they failed to carry it out and ended up as exiles being slaves again.

If the world carries on doing worse things like that, God will have to wipe it clean again with fire.

- - - - - - -

Satan, who is the god of this world, has blinded the minds of those who don't believe. They are unable to see the glorious light of the Good News. They don't understand this message about the glory of Christ, who is the exact likeness of God. 2 Corinthians ch.4 v4 (NLT)

Many people think that they are doing the right thing by going along with social media, watching television, slick presenters and most of the books calling for sexual intercourse, practising magic and following the idols. But they are mistaken. They are following Satan and we know what happens to Satan in the end (see Revelation ch.20 v10).

- - - - - - -

Even before he made the world, God loved us and chose us in Christ to be holy and without fault in his eyes. God decided in advance to adopt us into his own family by bringing us to himself through Jesus Christ. This is what he wanted to do, and it gave him great pleasure. Ephesians ch.1 v4-5 (NLT)

God knew all the time that man and women sinned. This is why he loved us and spared us. Before man had come along, he decided to send his Son, Jesus into the world (see Ephesians ch.2 v4-10), to redeem those whom he had chosen.

How good is the God that saved us, out off all the people in the world, from the past and the future? He called us by our name and he loved us.

- - - - - - -

For he has set a day when he will judge the world with justice by the man he has appointed. He has given proof of this to all man by raising him from the dead. Acts ch.17 v31

Jesus was only about thirty years old. He was arrested, he was beaten by the authorities, he was handed over to the Romans and crucified, hung on the cross with nails. He taught the truths of God, he healed the sick yet that wasn't enough. He was brought to the Sanhedrin by a traitor as a disciple and executed for us.

Jesus will be coming back to this world. Not in a manger but with a loud command and the trumpet call of God (see 1 Thessalonians ch.4 v16) and his good angels with him (see Revelation ch.19 v14). He will turn justice with fairness to all men who didn't believe in him. Their works will be brought under his judgement and his throne. God raised him from the dead and that is all the proof we need.

- - - - - - -

We are instructed to turn from godless living and sinful pleasures. We should live in this evil world with wisdom, righteousness, and devotion to God, while we look forward with hope to that wonderful day when the glory of our great God and Saviour, Jesus Christ, will be revealed. He gave his life to free us from every kind of sin, to cleanse us, and to make us his very own people, totally committed to doing good deeds. Titus ch.2 v12-14 (NLT)

Believers are instructed to turn from evil living and sinful pleasures. We should live in the world in the Holy Spirit doing what Jesus will want: with wisdom with righteousness as a devotion to God. Ready to look forward to Jesus he gave his life to free us, made us his own people and was committed to doing good for all.

The world was not worthy of them. They wandered about in deserts and mountains, and in caves and holes in the ground ... For here we do not have an enduring city, but we are looking for the city that is to come. Hebrews ch.11 v38; ch.13 v14

Most believers, known and unknown, who demonstrated their faith in God by persevering in the face of harsh trials and afflictions. They were outcasts, worthless people looking for their home in heaven. Many suffer the fate of being killed, tortured, jeers and flogging, and still waiting in prison. They didn't have anything to wear but wore sheepskins and goatskins. Still others wait; suffer the terrible effect on them and their families.

The world was not worthy of them. God watches over them and he knows their names.

- - - - - - -

Jesus Christ without blemish or defect ... He was chosen before the creation of the world. 1 Peter ch.1 v19-20

Jesus came to his own but they ignored him. All things were made by him, in him was life, the life was the light of men, but they didn't recognise him because they were surrounded by darkness. He was sinless (see 1 John ch.3 v5), but that didn't make any difference. He started life with the visit of the Magi and he ended his life in Jerusalem.

This was Jesus, but the world carried on and forgot about him. They doubted his miracles and they played down his healing. But the disciples understood his message and the church was started and will carry on with his presence, but the Holy Spirit will be there right to the end.

Listen! The Lord is coming with countless thousands of his holy ones to execute judgement on the people of the world. He will convict every person of all the ungodly things they have done and for all the insults that ungodly sinners have spoken against him. These people are grumblers and complainers, living only to satisfy their desires. They brag loudly about themselves, and they flatter others to get what they want. Jude ch.1 v14-16 (NLT)

Do not make a mistake. Jesus will be coming back and will judge the world. All the insults they made against him and his Father in heaven. This thunder and living scene and the awesome judgement that is depicted to emphasise the condemnation of the wicked. These men in the book of Jude and false teachers who pervert the grace of God. These godless men should not take the believers by surprise, for it had been predicted by the apostles in their letters to the churches.

WORRY

Worry has a cause to be anxious or to pester others.

Don't worry about your personal belongings, for the best of all the land of Egypt is yours. Genesis ch.45 v20 (NLT)

Joseph was a slave in Egypt but he was second in line to Pharaoh (see Genesis ch.41 v40). Joseph gave out the crops to the starving people. Jacob heard about it and wanted to go and see his son Joseph (see Genesis ch.45 v28). When they came to Egypt the best of the land even the land of Goshen. Said Joseph, 'You don't have to worry about the belongings, the best of the land is yours'. Just take it.

- - - - - - -

But you are obsessed with whether the godless will be judged. Don't worry, judgement and justice will be upheld. Job ch.36 v17 (NLT)

After the three friends had explained what Job had done, they didn't have anything to say to him. He was silent whilst the other friend spoke and Elihu became angry with Job for justifying himself rather than God (see Job ch.32 v2). He was annoyed because Job was not trying to make God important. Elihu said judgement and justice will be confirmed and vindicated, so God will call everybody to account for what they had done.

The worry about the problems of the earth will be dealt with by God himself.

- - - - - - -

Don't worry about the wicked or envy those who do wrong. For like grass, they soon fade away. Like spring flowers, they soon wither. Psalm ch.37 v1-2 (NLT)

Just remember, the things of earth will soon be gone. Many people look back in history, they don't remember the trouble and waste will be around for ages. God is in control and he is not willing to let the earth be ruined, through Satan or by anybody else.

Worry weighs a person down; an encouraging word cheers a person up. Proverbs ch.12 v25 (NLT)

Any protesters that will worry, make their job very difficult with how to balance their lives with what is happening today. They need to get noticed, they feel that it is important to be recognised, regardless of the family around them. They even take children to protest about the things they are interested in. They would not even notice how bad they sound to many.

This shows that the protesters needn't worry. It has been going on for thousands of years and many things will need to be changed.

But the start is for you, do you know and understand that the Lord Jesus is calling you to change from to sinful nature that you have, to appreciate that you have sinned and come short of what God expects? Jesus is reminding you that that what he expects for you to do (see Matthew ch.11 v28-30). He reminds you that you must be saved. Then only when you have done this then you can see clearly again. The route is simple, you have to change, then the others will change also.

This is what cheers the person up and makes him see what is going on.

- - - - - - -

This tells us that the world is a sad, sorry place and nothing will be gained until the Jesus takes overall command (see Revelation ch.22 v10-11).

Therefore I tell you, do not worry about your life, what you will eat or drink; or about your body what you will wear. Matthew ch.6 v25

The believer is patient but he does not believe that things will improve. Jesus said: 'Do not worry about your life. What you will eat? What you will drink? What you will wear? Seek first his kingdom and his righteousness and all these things will be given to you as well' (see Matthew ch.6 v33). Righteous living will be there to guide you in what you should be doing, not wanting to eat, drink and what to wear. There are more important things you should be doing, 'seek first his kingdom'. Do you know what it means?

When a body dies, they will go the Hades (the waiting place) and will wait until the judgement from God. But if a person repents and came to Jesus, he will have his name written in the book of life which means he is a child of God. This is what Jesus means 'his kingdom'.

- - - - - - -

When ever you are arrested and brought to trial; do not worry beforehand about what to say. Just say whatever is given you at that time, for it is not you speaking, but the Holy Spirit. Mark ch.13 v11

Whenever you are arrested, the Holy Spirit will give you answers for that time. Don't worry, about what you will say to those who interrogate you. Just respond to what the Holy Spirit will remind you. You will be arrested and thrown into prison because the Holy Spirit will say the things that a normal person wouldn't. Destitute, persecuted and ill-treated but you will be honoured by God who sees all things (see Hebrews ch.11).

- - - - - - -

Yes, each of you should remain as you were when God called you. Are you a slave? Don't let that worry you—but if you get a chance to be free, take it. 1 Corinthians ch.7 v20-21 (NLT)

Perhaps you were a slave, but there are more valuable and important things to do. This is much more important than even living your life. Whether you are a slave be there and talk with the slaves around you, if you are a free man go out and tell the world what Jesus had done for you.

Jesus said, "I tell you the truth, anyone who will not receive the kingdom of God like a little child, will never enter it." Mark ch.10 v15

It is so simple that even a child could understand it.

- - - - - - -

Don't worry about anything; instead, pray about everything. Tell God what you need, and thank him for all he has done. Then you will experience God's peace, which exceeds anything we can understand. Philippians ch.4 v6-7 (NLT)

The believer will pray to God and thank him for what he has done. Then you can experience God's peace which comes freely to you. This is more than could be achieved by the world's system.

Peace: God rewarded Phinehas, son of Aaron, because he was zealous for the Lord and turned God's anger away from the Israelites. God made peace with him, his peace is like a stillness and restfulness, a quietness, silence and contentment (see Numbers ch.25 v11-12). Nobody could imagine what

God's peace is like.

- - - - - - -

Now, who will want to harm you if you are eager to do good? But even if you suffer for doing what is right, God will reward you for it. So don't worry or be afraid of their threats. 1 Peter ch.3 v13-14 (NLT)

God is watching you, contemplating you, thinking about you. God will reward you for what you have done. It is only a small a minor thing but God notices. He will present you with a reward when you arrive at the judgement. So don't be worried about the threats on your life; nobody could take away your soul. God looks after your soul and you will be with him forever. God is more important than anything else, whether you are a protester or not.